Play-acting

Luke Dixon is a director, teacher and academic. He is internationally known for both productions of Shakespeare and site-specific work. He has run workshops and training programmes in Asia, Africa, North and South America, throughout Europe as well as in the UK. His doctoral thesis was in the performance of gender and he has published widely on that subject as well as on multilingual and multicultural performance. Luke is Artistic Director of Theatre Nomad and the International Workshop Festival.

Play-acting

A guide to theatre workshops

LUKE DIXON

Methuen Drama

Published by Methuen Drama

10 9 8 7 6 5 4 3 2

First published in 2003 by
Methuen Publishing Limited

Methuen Drama
A & C Black Publishers Limited
38 Soho Square
London W1D 3HB

A CIP catalogue record for this book is available
from the British Library.

ISBN 978 0 413 77294 7

Designed by Helen Ewing

Typeset by SX Composing DTP, Rayleigh, Essex
Printed and bound in Great Britain by
MPG Books Ltd, Bodmin, Cornwall

For Harriet, Will and Sid

Contents

Illustrations

Acknowledgements

Many people have contributed to the making of this book, some knowingly, many unknowingly.

I have had conversations before, during and after workshops, with Segun Adefila, Carmen Maja Antoni, Eugenio Barba, Jane Boston, Pippa Bound, Ivan Cartwright, Clare Davidson, Robert Davidson, John Fox, Sue Gill, Andy Grewar, Greg Hicks, Katsura Kan, Jo King, Tyrone Landau, Glenn Lee, John Laher, André Lemmer, Zwai Mgwima, Winston Ntshona, Yoshi Oida, Janice Perry, Ramiro Silveira, Sue Smith, Joshua Sofaer, Ana Tamen, Carlo Alexandre Teixeira and Birte Twisselmann.

I have had a lifetime of working relationships with other theatre makers who have between them influenced all of my creative practice. The designer Paul Dart opened my imagination to the possibilities of theatrical space. With David Baird, Noël Greig, Becky Hall and Jane Turner I have made theatre and led magical workshops. Their influence will become clear as you read this book.

And I have worked with wonderful performers, most especially the actors of Theatre Nomad with whom I have travelled the globe as I have written this book and who have given me great practical help: Louise Barrett, Paola Cavallin, Victoria Gillmon, Steven Hobson, Paul Huntley-Thomas, Andrea Molnár, Jean Pagni, Amanda Palmer, Lisa Payne, Laure Salama and Karola Timm.

My colleagues at the International Workshop Festival – Kathy Everett, Jeremy Smeeth and Sebastian Warrack – have never complained when my attention has diverted from the Festival to this book.

Liz Turner has always been quietly supportive behind every theatrical project, the perfect administrator, colleague and friend. I hope this book goes some way to acknowledging her faith in me all these years.

Though I started writing this book at the University of Port Elizabeth in South Africa, it only really came to life while talking with Patsy Rodenburg on a train journey to Brighton. She it was who put me in touch with Methuen. At Methuen Max Eilenberg saw how my collection of writings might be made into a book and Elizabeth Ingrams was an incisive and challenging editor.

Preface

In the little settlement of Fitches Corner on the edge of the vast desert that is the South African Karoo, the whole community had turned out to entertain me and the small troupe of actors with which I was on tour. The performance lasted about an hour. Never had we been so entertained. We were five actors from five different European countries (Norway, Germany, France, England, Italy) and me, an English director. It was our first experience of Africa. As we showed our appreciation and delight in what we had witnessed, the local arts worker asked if we could help develop the performance skills of the community. Would we run a theatre workshop for the entire village? And so there and then under a blazing sun on parched grass we brought everyone together and set to work.

There was little English spoken in the village – let alone Norwegian, French, Italian or German – and any instruction had to be translated into Xhosa, the local language. So we decided to run a workshop that was, as far as possible, entirely without words. Our lack of a common language was to be turned to our advantage. I started with a children's game that we had used in hundreds of different ways – grandmother's footsteps; it is explained in detail later in the book. For me the game has always been central to finding ways of making cross-cultural connections. Everywhere we had travelled – from the Canadian Rockies to the plains of Siberia – we had found the game to be played. Our French actor, Jean Pagni, was the grandmother and as he turned his back an African village advanced towards him. Every time he turned to face the villagers he would send back to the starting point those he caught moving. Names were learned quickly amid the laughter. Eventually, someone from the village touched Jean without being caught moving and took his place. Now we played the game competitively in groups, each European actor with about a dozen villagers. Through sign and expression, strategies were worked out. In their different ways each group moved as one and we played until all collapsed in giggles and laughter.

Then Paola Cavallin took over with something entirely different and from a specific European tradition. Born and trained in Venice, she is a great and passionate exponent of Italian *commedia dell'arte*. The village and the actors formed one giant circle and she took everyone through the movements, sounds and expressions of three archetypal *commedia* characters, including her beloved Pantelone. We all adopted, detail by detail, the physical characteristics of each character and then advanced towards the centre of the circle and out again. Then we took suggestions from our hosts for archetypes from their own culture and were soon policemen and tribal chiefs. The attention and the exquisite detailing of the physical work were astonishing. Finally, we all returned to the favourite of the characters we had explored and paraded around the village. And there, as the sun blazed from an African sky on to the dry grass of the remote little settlement of Fitches Corner, sixty African Pantelones caused laughter and delight.

In little over an hour we had become an ensemble of performers, united in the shared enjoyment of the games we were playing, exploring the physicality of acting, the creation of character and the making of performance.

The workshop in the African bush was with an itinerant group of actors – the nomads of Theatre Nomad – with whom I have travelled the world. It is just one example of hundreds. The actors of the company live across the globe and as we travel we find new performers to work with. Though we have based ourselves in different locations over the years, we come together wherever a tour or a project takes us, a loose team of theatre makers grouping and regrouping around the world. Wherever we have given performances we have also run workshops, both to share our skills and to learn new ones. We have run workshops in universities in North America, drama schools in England, with theatre companies across the globe, in community settings in Africa, high in the Bavarian Alps and on the beaches of the Indian Ocean. We have worked with students, schoolchildren and teachers, with dancers and with opera singers, with experienced actors and with novices. Many of those workshops were in response to specific situations. Some were to develop skills, others to explore texts or characters. Some were to create performance, others to engage audiences with performances they had seen. Some workshops were little more than an hour long; others extended over days, even weeks. All were about the teaching, sharing and exchanging of the skills and techniques of acting.

It was perhaps the English director Joan Littlewood who invented the term 'theatre workshop' in the 1950s. Littlewood's workshop was an ensemble, a radical movement and a method of creating entire shows. Half a century later the term 'theatre workshop' is used to cover a wide variety of activities happening in many different circumstances and in many different time frames. For this book I have brought together workshops that fulfil the function of that in the African village, teaching, sharing and exchanging skills and techniques of acting.

A workshop can be the very engine room of theatrical creativity, a place where an actor, teacher or director is at their most vulnerable, most exposed, most powerful and most creative. A place where anything can happen and all is possible. It is where theatre is made. It is beyond rehearsal. The theatre workshop is not about remaking, it is about original creativity, the making of theatre itself. It is a way of unleashing the raw creative process of acting and theatre making and using that to train, develop skills and make performances.

The workshop is at the heart of contemporary theatre practice. It is, in its different forms, the primary method of both training and of theatre making, and as such is the tool by which actors learn their craft, teachers pass on that craft and directors develop it in production.

This book brings together in one programme a multitude of theatre workshops developed over years in every possible directing and teaching situation to guide actors and groups of actors to many different goals. Just like the workshop in Africa, they can help to bring together a group of actors and build an ensemble, create and develop character, explore ideas, themes and situations, exchange ideas and extend an actor's range and skills. Each workshop is complete in itself and can be used in any number of situations. Some you may return to again and again, others use only once.

WHAT'S IN IT FOR ME?
If you follow this book as an actor, you will be taken through a practical programme. By the end you will know how your body

works and the ways in which you can use it in performance. You will know how your voice functions in relation to your body and to the words that you speak. And you will have found ways in which your mind and imagination can be used in the creation of characters and the theatrical worlds they inhabit. Workshops are almost by definition group activities, and while many of these exercises can be used by you the actor working on your own, ideally you should find friends or colleagues (often just a partner will suffice) to work with you through the entire programme.

If you follow this book as a teacher, you will have a manual that can be held in your hand during class, providing a structured programme of work, the sections of which can be used as they are or with your own variations.

If you follow this book as a director, you will have a structured approach to a rehearsal process – whether for staging a text or devising a new piece of work. You can use the series of workshops as a pre-rehearsal process to build an ensemble of actors able to work at their best both individually and as a group.

HOW TO USE THIS BOOK

The book consists of thirty-two self-contained but linked workshops. The programme takes you on a journey from learning about the anatomy of the individual actor's body to the performance of narrative by a group of actors. Each workshop contains a series of instructions to performers – words to say to others or to hear yourself. These instructions can be read by one voice or by many. Workshops do not have to be led by just one person. I have often run workshops with others and some of my co-leaders make their appearances in this book. The workshop instructions are supplemented by observations as to what you might expect to experience as an actor or as a teacher or director, and with ideas as to how to exploit and develop unexpected opportunities. There is also guidance as to how the work might be applied to specific situations.

No two workshops are ever the same. The workshops in this book are templates to be added to and subtracted from as needs arise. All have come from practical experience and though many may appear simple, they are a response to complex ideas and difficult challenges.

Make these workshops your own. Pay attention to the space

you are using and how it is contained, whether you are working indoors or out. Will you use all of the space physically available to you or only part of it? Are the doors, if there are doors, to be open or closed? What distractions might there be? How will you light the space? Should the participants wear shoes or socks or have bare feet? Is the space warm enough?

Find out all you can about your group, even if only in the first few minutes of the workshop. This might be through introduction and conversation or it may be through the setting of a simple task. Remember that a workshop group is made up of individuals, each of whom will experience something different from the others and all of whom will be having a different experience from you. If you are repeating a workshop with a new group, remember that, however familiar it is to you, it will all be new to them.

Keep an eye on the clock. The length of a workshop is dependent upon many factors, only some of which might be under your control. Each of these workshops needs at least ninety minutes or two hours to run its course without hurry. Many (such as the labyrinth or the storytelling workshops) can easily be extended to a day, two days, even a week. If you are teaching this book as a programme, you should find enough material in each workshop for all of your workshops to be of a similar length. Plan how to use your time and plan for a clear conclusion, a finish that will end the workshop on a positive, creative note and a sense of achievement within the group.

Enjoy silence during a workshop. Much may be happening without there being any sound. Give thought to how you break the silence before a workshop begins, through speaking, atmosphere or music.

Always warm up. Trust yourself, trust the group and trust the workshop. Something will happen.

Part One
BODY AND VOICE

Introduction

We walk before we talk. Before we can walk we have to learn to stand. So it should be with learning to perform and so this first section starts with the body before moving on to the voice. The early workshops explore the performer's body, examining it, feeling it, searching for its potential and eventually putting it into movement in the workshop space.

Play is the thing and these workshops take the performer back to a world of play, of childhood freedom of expression and of intuition. The programme encourages the performer to relearn what has been unlearned in conventional education. The work develops physical memory. With the freedom of the return to childhood comes a release from habit, from the ways of using the body that the performer will have picked up over their lifetime, to find the balance, the centre, the magic neutrality of the unencumbered performer from which anything is possible.

Speaking and listening are physical activities. All the voice work in this section comes from an understanding of the functioning of the performer's body, of which the voice is just one extraordinary part. We start with breathing, the activity that keeps the body alive and gives it motion, and the activity that is the basis for all voice work. We explore the infinite variety possible in the use of just one or two simple words before going on to sentences, verse and more complex forms of expression. The voice is constantly explored in relation to the moving actor and the dynamic relationship between body, voice and space.

Chapter One
THE FOOT

We are going to start with our feet. The foot is often neglected, yet it is literally the basis of all performance. The foot is one of the most evolutionarily advanced parts of our anatomy and like the hand separates us from our fellow animals. The bones in our feet connect us to the ground we walk on, the world we inhabit and the stage we perform on. The foot is the most complicated collection of bones and joints in our body. Yet we think little about our feet and have only a rudimentary understanding of what it is they do and how they work. As most of the workshops in this book require the use of our feet, we will start by spending some time getting to know them.

Work in pairs or on your own.

Massage your partner's foot or your own.

There are twenty-eight bones in each foot and a whole complexity of joints holding them together and articulating them.

How many of those bones can you feel?

How are they articulated?

Separate out the bones.

This is an intimate workshop with which to begin and in some situations it might be better to work individually rather than in pairs. But like all body work, indeed all performance work, so much more is to be gained from working in tandem or in groups, feeling and being felt, observing and being observed, acting and reacting.

Find a piece of paper and a pencil.

Choose a foot. Your own or your partner's.

Draw an outline of your chosen foot.

Make a mark at the midpoint of each side.

Join the marks.

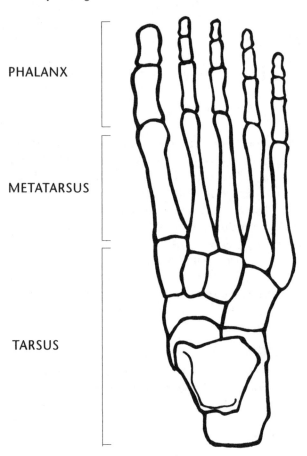

PHALANX

METATARSUS

TARSUS

Bones of the foot

The back half is made up of the seven tarsal bones. The front half is made up of the long bones – the metatarsals and the phalanges. These end in the toes but start in the middle of your foot. This is one of the most complicated collection of bones and joints in our body. The feet are for weight bearing and balance. Our entire body weight is borne by the base bones on each foot – these are the taluses. The talus spreads the weight, half back into the heel and half forward into the two sesamoids of metatarsal 1 and to metatarsals 2–5; so our big toe takes twice the weight of our other toes. When we walk our weight starts at the heel and spreads forward along each outside edge to the metatarsal heads.

A lot of theory to start with, but our feet are the beginning and end of all our work, supporting our entire performance.

> Return to the outlines of your feet.
>
> Stand on them.
>
> The line between the two halves of each foot shows a line of balance. Half the weight of your entire body is borne in front of these lines. Half the weight is borne behind the lines.
>
> Shift your balance.
>
> Rock to and fro.
>
> Find your perfect point of balance.
>
> Have someone else help you find it.
>
> How little movement is there and from where can that balance shift?
>
> Search for your centre.
>
> Find a point of perfect balance with your body in neutral.

Reflexologists work from the theory that energy flows through channels within the body connecting every organ and gland to an ending or pressure point in the foot. Massaging the appropriate reflex points on the soles of the feet can clear blocked energy channels, restore energy flow and so promote healing and well-being. Massaging your toes can benefit your sinuses; the area between the tips of your toes and your feet affects your eyes, ears, neck and throat (perhaps this is why things we see and hear 'make our toes curl'). The centre of the front of your foot affects your lungs, and so on.

> Return to your foot or that of your partner.
>
> Now that you are more aware of how the feet are constructed, gently massage them again and open yourself to responses from elsewhere in your body.

Allow time for this. It is an opportunity for relaxation and reflection after so much theory, and a time for close pair work, for

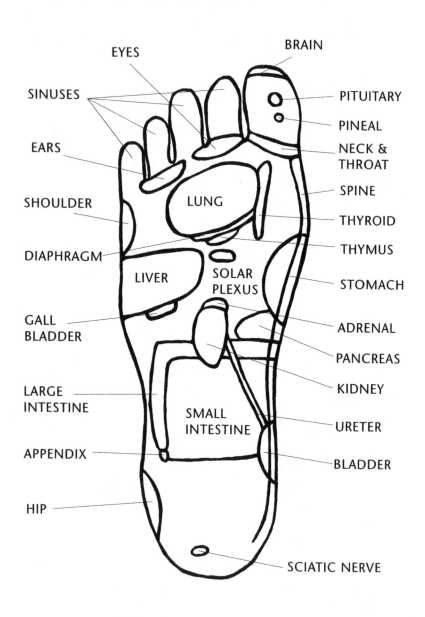

EYES

BRAIN

SINUSES

PITUITARY

PINEAL

EARS

NECK &
THROAT

SHOULDER

SPINE

LUNG

THYROID

DIAPHRAGM

THYMUS

LIVER

SOLAR
PLEXUS

STOMACH

GALL
BLADDER

ADRENAL

PANCREAS

KIDNEY

LARGE
INTESTINE

SMALL
INTESTINE

URETER

APPENDIX

BLADDER

HIP

SCIATIC NERVE

Reflexology points (right foot)

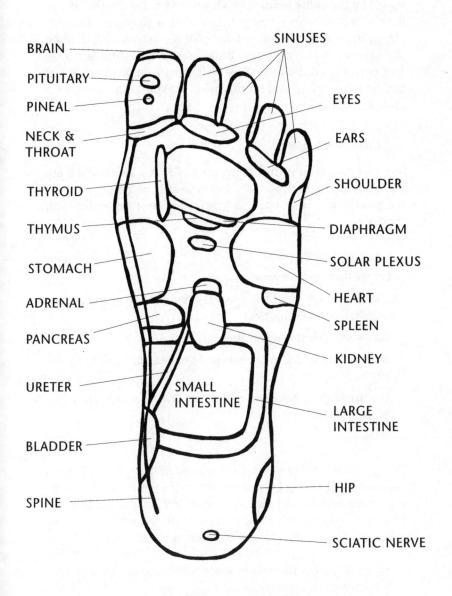

BRAIN

PITUITARY

PINEAL

NECK & THROAT

THYROID

THYMUS

STOMACH

ADRENAL

PANCREAS

URETER

BLADDER

SPINE

SINUSES

EYES

EARS

SHOULDER

DIAPHRAGM

SOLAR PLEXUS

HEART

SPLEEN

KIDNEY

SMALL INTESTINE

LARGE INTESTINE

HIP

SCIATIC NERVE

Reflexology points (left foot)

feedback and discussion. The feedback can be within pairs or shared by the entire group. Do whatever feels appropriate. If you have a large enough group you can sit in a circle and ask each person to cross one leg on to the lap of the person next to them and explore and massage each other's feet in a continuous circle. This is an opportunity for all participants to simultaneously feel and be felt, explore and be explored, working collectively on a very personal task.

STANDING UP

So far we have been sitting on the floor. Now it's time to stand up. We are going to do this slowly and only after becoming aware of the ground that we will be standing on and our relationship with the floor.

> Lie on your back.
>
> Let the floor support you.
>
> Spread yourself; melt to the floor. Let the floor do all the work of support. Free your muscles.
>
> Turn your mind to your breathing.
>
> Relax your head and your neck; find the best possible passage for air.
>
> Do absolutely nothing, so that when you do something it has absolute clarity.
>
> Relax.

Doing nothing, being neutral, is the most difficult challenge for a performer, yet neutrality and inactivity, the erasure of character, is the essential starting point for activity and performing. Through this and subsequent workshops we will return to ways of achieving the starting point of the neutral performer.

> Scan your body – this will become a regular and familiar activity as these workshops progress.
>
> Become familiar with doing nothing.
>
> Slowly move your heels to your bottom.

Your knees become suspended.

Keep a comfortable distance between your feet.

Feel the weight of your knees and your pelvis pouring into the floor.

Open the surface of the foot. Make real contact with the floor.

Slide the feet along the floor backwards and forwards. Feel the articulation in your knees and hips.

Then let the knees fall to one side.

Let the top foot slide away and then swing it over the other until you begin to roll on to your side; don't lose touch with the floor.

Then swing back.

Bring the knees up again.

Drop them the other way.

Repeat the exercise on the other side.

Roll over so that you are kneeling and sitting on your haunches.

Now the tops of your feet should be in contact with the floor, your buttocks on your heels.

Articulate your feet. Work them into close contact with the floor from the top.

When you are ready, stand up. *Homo erectus.*

Use those fifty-six bones to support yourself. Keep that contact with the floor.

Pour yourself into your feet.

In the 1960s, Eugenio Barba, the director and theorist, picked up his feet and went from his home in the south of Italy to Poland, where he joined forces for a while with Jerzy Grotowski. From there they took him to Denmark where he founded his Odin Teatret and his International School of Theatre Anthropology, linking study of society and culture with that of performance.

Eugenio leads workshops in which the action is focused entirely on the foot. With him I have performed complete scenes from *Hamlet* using just one of my feet and one belonging to my workshop partner, the German actress Karola Timm. Barba's exercise is a useful rehearsal tool and also indicates the possibilities that can come from the precise and detailed use of every part of your body.

Chapter Two

CONNECTING THE BONES

The God of the Old Testament took hold of Ezekiel and carried him off through the skies, setting him down in a valley full of bones. Recounting his experience, Ezekiel says that 'there were very many bones in the open valley; and, lo, they were very dry'. Ezekiel called on the Lord to bring the bones to life and as He did so, 'There was a noise, and behold a shaking, and the bones came together, bone to his bone.' The American songwriter James Weldon Johnson, writer of 'The Negro National Anthem', composed for Abraham Lincoln's birthday, and a major figure in the Harlem renaissance, a popular song about Ezekiel and his experiences in the valley of bones. It is a song still sung by people everywhere:

> Ezekiel connected dem dry bones
> Ezekiel connected dem dry bones
> Ezekiel connected dem dry bones
> I hear the word of the Lord.
> Your toe bone connected to your foot bone,
> Your foot bone connected to your ankle bone,
> Your ankle bone connected to your leg bone,
> Your leg bone connected to your knee bone,
> Your knee bone connected to your thigh bone,
> Your thigh bone connected to your hip bone,
> Your hip bone connected to your back bone,
> Your back bone connected to your shoulder bone,
> Your shoulder bone connected to your neck bone,
> Your neck bone connected to your head bone,
> I hear the word of the Lord!
> Now hear the word of the Lord.
> Dem bones, dem bones gonna walk aroun'
> Dem bones, dem bones gonna walk aroun'
> Dem bones, dem bones gonna walk aroun'
> I hear the word of the Lord!

The song could be used as an *aide-mémoire* in this workshop, as we play with the workings of the skeleton and the ways in which the body is articulated. As we join up our bones and make them walk around, we will begin again with the feet. Not the one-foot bone of the song but the bones of the feet that we discovered in the last workshop.

Find a space. Stand comfortably. Stretch.

Stretching is vital to the performer. A full stretch of every part of the body is a prerequisite of any warm-up and integral to many of these physical workshops. Different actors will have different ways of stretching and different exercises that they find useful for their own bodies and even a group warm-up should allow time for that individuality. But a guided group stretch is often useful to ensure that nothing is missed and that laziness and habit do not creep in.

This is a very gentle stretch, a limber to get the body moving and oxygenate the muscles and articulate the joints. It is a stretch I like to use to focus and energise when performers are tired or inexperienced or have not been working for a while. Any workshop participant should easily do it. Some work and workshops will demand a much more vigorous and extensive stretch over a longer period of time and in detail on those parts of the body about to be put into action. However, for most of the work in this programme, this is a good basic stretch.

STRETCH

Stand comfortably with legs apart. Centre yourself. Be balanced.

Breathe in. Breathe out.

Breathe in and reach up.

Breathe out and let your arms down and relax.

Breathe in and reach up again, further this time.

Breathe out and come down and relax.

Now do the same with just the right arm.

Breathe in and reach up.

Breathe out and come down and relax.

Breathe in and reach up further.

Breathe out and come down and relax.

Now repeat this with the left arm.

Inhale as you stretch up.

Exhale as you relax and come down.

Now repeat this with the right arm.

Inhale as you stretch up. Exhale as you relax and come down.

Inhale and stretch both arms up. Exhale and bring your arms and body down so your hands touch the floor, bending your knees as you do so.

With your arms hanging down, move from your hips.

Swing. Bend your knees and loosen your back.

Now begin to come up. Build up through the vertebrae.

Walk your fingers up your back as you do this.

Then repeat. Inhale and exhale.

As you breathe out, relax your back and fall forward so your hands touch the floor again.

Walk your hands out a little. And walk your hands back.

With your arms hanging to the ground, draw a figure of eight on the floor with your hands. First one way, then the other.

Alternately straighten your legs as you go.

Draw the figure of eight on the floor. Be led by your coccyx.

Return to centre, return to upright and relax.

Take your weight over on to your right leg, by pushing with your left. Make the same change on the move back.

Bring your arms down to the floor, walk them to centre, uncoil your back, and come over on to your left leg by pushing up straight on your right.

We are going to move our hips.

Imagine there is a hoop around you. Move your hips so as to touch every part of that hoop.

Move the hoop up your body and do the same with your tummy.

First clockwise, then anti-clockwise. Then up to your neck.

Now corkscrew up and down from neck to tummy to hips and back again.

Shake out.

All of these muscles we have been using are connected to the bones in our skeleton and it is the contraction and relaxation of the muscles that puts those bones and our bodies into motion. The next part of the workshop identifies the parts of the body and the skeleton inside it. Firstly with the actors working on their own, then in pairs and eventually in larger groups.

ARTICULATING THE BODY

Stand comfortably in the space. Relax.

Release the tensions in your major joints – knees, hips, shoulders, elbow, and wrists.

Push against the floor. You know about your feet.

Articulate as many of the joints in your left foot as you can.

Wriggle your toes. Rock gently on the balls of the foot.

Pull up your instep. Relax.

Push with your big toe. Then your little toe.

Now your right foot. Now both feet together.

Let the movement travel from your feet up your body. Into your ankles. How much movement is there in that joint?

Become aware of its complexity and potential. Stand on tiptoes.

Pick up one leg and rotate the foot.

Then the other. Flex and bend that ankle in every which way.

So through the shins to the knees. Again experiment with the possibilities of movement. Bend and straighten, twist, rotate and point.

On through the thighs into the hips. The hips join our legs to the rest of our body.

Start with the left. Increase the amount of movement.

To the front, to the back, to the left, to the right.

Move yourself up and down. Then the right. Then both together.

Keep the rest of the feet and legs moving as well.

The spine is so important that we will devote a whole workshop to it. So next:

Move through the spine and into the shoulders. The shoulders are hanging from your spine.

Start with the left.

Raise, lower and rotate the shoulder.

Feel your back and neck move as you move your shoulder. Now take the movement down from the shoulder through the arms and into the elbow.

Let the forearm and elbow hang loose.

How much movement is possible? And in which directions?

Now move through the forearm to the wrist.

Then from the wrist into the hands and the fingers.

From your shoulder to your fingertips.

Everything should be in movement, in every direction and dimension. Relax and move to the right shoulder. Make the same journey to the fingertips of the right hand.

The hand is supremely important in many Asian theatre traditions, where the slightest, most delicate of movements of a finger, palm or wrist can convey a wealth of meaning. One of the few artists to survive the regime of Pol Pot in Cambodia was Em Theay. She is one of the great exponents of classical Khmer dance where a performer spends a lifetime devoted to just one of the primary roles of female, male, giant and monkey. Uniquely, Em Theay is able to interpret not one but all. Watching this remarkable eighty-year-old woman teach at the Royal University of Fine Art in Phnom Penh revealed to me, as never before, just how important the use of the hands can be in conveying everything you need to know about character, mood and situation. Western theatre takes

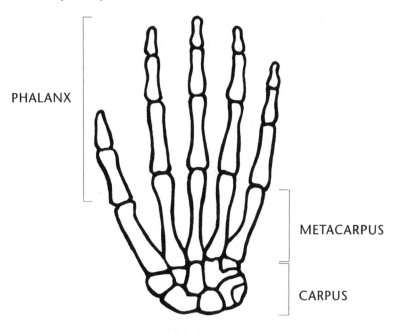

PHALANX

METACARPUS

CARPUS

Bones of the hand

much less notice of the hand, to the extent that actors often complain that they do not know what to do with their hands. The hand was once a foot; its release from the ground and our ability to stand upright distinguishes us as humans. The hand, no longer needed for walking, became prehensile, able to grasp and hold things. Unlike the foot, the hand is wonderfully articulate and the thumb is the most articulate part of the hand, able to touch the palm and the tips of all the fingers.

THE HAND

With a partner explore your hands.

Start with the palm.

The mobility of our hand, its prehensile qualities, is one of the things that make us human. Even our palm is extremely mobile. There are thirteen bones in each of our palms, all of which articulate with each other and with the forearm in extremely complex ways. The eight closely interlinked bones at the wrist make up the carpus. From the carpus to the fingers are the five long bones of the metacarpus.

> Feel for as many bones as you can. Explore their movement with each other.
>
> Explore how they move with the wrist. Explore how they lead to the fingers.

This is difficult to do because of the strong fibrous membrane under the skin, the palmar aponeurosis, which covers the palm.

Now we move from the palm to the fingers. Each finger has three bones, the phalanges, united, like the Greek and Macedonian fighters after which they are named, for a common purpose. The thumb has two.

> Articulate each finger.
>
> How and where can it move?
>
> Articulate the thumb.

The joining of the thumb to the palm is the one thing about our body more than anything else that makes us human and has allowed for the development of our culture, enabling us to write, to paint, to cultivate the soil and to build.

> Flatten the thumb on to the palm of the hand.
>
> Touch the tip and the base of each finger with the thumb. No other animal can do that.
>
> Play with your hands.
>
> Find out what they are capable of.

We have taken time out to work on the hands, so now relax, centre, balance and return to articulating the body.

> Articulate your whole body from the feet up.
>
> Through your feet into your legs and so on up through the body and down through the arms.

As you articulate a new part of the body, through 'dem bones', the rest of your body that has already been worked on should be in a state of constant minimal movement, keeping the energy running through your body.

And so to the neck and up to the top of the spine that disappears into and supports the skull.

Move your head and articulate your jaw.

Play with the movements possible through all of your body.

Encourage your participants to use the tiniest of movements and the most extreme of movements with everything in between. Always use control and careful transition. Slowly bring the group to stillness.

POSES AND PUPPETS

Find a partner.

From the feet, build your partner bone by bone.

Gently move from one bone and joint to the next, softly manipulating them as if assembling the body.

Be relaxed but still as this is done to you.

Explore by touch and observation all that you have felt within yourself. Feet, shins, knees, thighs, hips, spine, shoulders, arms, elbows, forearms, wrists, hands, fingers, neck, skull and jaw. Discover with your partner how your body is built.

Swap over, relax, discuss.

Using your partner as a puppet, create a series of poses.

Start with the limbs.

Then the fingers.

Then the neck and head.

Then the face.

Swap over.

The German artist Marianne Wex undertook a major work about human posture when she brought together, in the 'Neue

Gesellschaft für Bildende Kunst' in Berlin, some 6,000 photographs of body postures. For Wex this huge display demonstrated that body language is the result of sex-based, patriarchal socialisation. She took her project further when in 1979 she published a book not only of her photographs but also of photographs of sculptures drawn from 4,000 years of Western art, with thousands of different possible poses. Working with real bodies in three dimensions it should be possible to find thousands more. Use the following exercise to explore posture and the ways in which the body can be placed in space and the different things that can be indicated with the pose. You can say things about gender, period and culture, create any theatrical world all by the poses you make.

Move your puppet partner in the space.

Interact with the other puppets.

Bunraku, the Japanese puppetry, inspires the next part of the workshop. Puppetry is an ancient tradition in Japan going back to the early nomadic *kugutsu-mawashi*, the 'puppet turners' of Central Asia. The puppets of bunraku are almost life-size and are each manipulated by three puppeteers. The chief puppeteer wears traditional eighteenth-century dress while the two assistants are covered in black with hoods over their heads, like Auditor who listens to Mouth in Beckett's *Not I*.

Work in groups of four like the manipulators of the bunraku theatre.

One person in the group is the puppet; the other three are puppeteers.

Decide who controls which parts of the human puppet.

Take time to stand out to look at the pose.

Move your puppet in the space.

Gradually learn to work with just the slightest touch.

Eventually you may be able to work with no touch at all; articulating your puppet as if with imaginary strings or sticks from increasing distances within the room.

You might want to introduce character or narrative at this stage. If you have more than one group, let the puppets interact.

Work slowly and carefully. Work with precision and observation.

Work as a team. Each of you, who are moving the puppet, take a stick. They can be of any length and all of different lengths. Garden canes or bamboo are ideal. With all the puppeteers gently touching one point on the puppet at the same time, manipulate your puppet with the sticks. Only one person moves at any one time, with all the puppeteers manipulating the same point on the puppet body.

In two groups and with two puppets, create a short narrative.

Start simply with archetypes that all the manipulators will know – a prince meets a princess, say, or two gods fight for power, and develop a simple narrative. If you are working on a text, create characters from that text with your human puppets. You may also find other methods of manipulation. I have watched the Thai director Teerawat Mulvilai working with the puppet actors being controlled from just a forefinger and thumb on the back of the neck around the seventh vertebra, in the manner of traditional Thai puppetry.

In the jungles of Cambodia, the shadow puppet masters embody the characters of the puppets they are manipulating. The connections of the translucent bearskin puppets are replicated in the movements of the puppeteers to the point where puppet and puppeteer are one. As characters engage in battle, the puppets can even be abandoned as the puppeteers themselves physicalise the story. Play with this concept as a way to finish the workshop, with a few archetypal characters and fluidity between puppet and puppeteers. The members of the National Theatre of Cambodia demonstrated this to me in the burned-out shell of their theatre in Phnom Penh. Two puppeteers began a battle of the gods behind the screen with the orchestra playing to their side. As the fight became more furious, puppeteers and puppets came in front of the screen, both in full view of their lone spectator. The puppeteers were making exactly the same moves as their two-dimensional puppets. Only the hands and arms, which held the puppets above their heads, were differently placed. As the battle grew to a climax, the puppets were laid to one side and the sequence ended with the puppeteers in three-dimensional martial artistry.

Chapter Three

THE SPINE

We all defy gravity. From the moment we get out of bed in the morning until the moment we return to it at night, we spend our time fighting to stay vertical. Three hundred thousand years ago our ancestor *Homo erectus* stood upright for the first time on the savannahs of Africa. Every day we mimic that first upright stance as we use our bodies in a way that sets us apart from our fellow animals, bringing our heads up into the world, taking our two front limbs from the task of walking and freeing them for other tasks. Man is a vertical being and the actor constantly plays with the dynamics involved in maintaining that position.

It is not easy to stand upright, yet it is something we do every day with little conscious thought. An understanding of how we function in the upright is essential to the efficient use of the actor's body and a realisation of its potential.

Frederick Alexander came to realise how crucial this understanding was in the early part of the twentieth century and his ideas are now a commonplace in the training, care and health of Western actors. Alexander was born in Tasmania in 1869 and became a professional elocutionist and reciter in Australia. Increasingly, he found his voice failing him in performance, yet doctors could find nothing wrong with him physically. Long periods of self-examination, watching himself perform in front of a mirror, convinced Alexander that it was muscular tension that was causing his problems. He developed a technique, the Alexander technique, to improve balance, coordination and relaxation, and by 1930 had his own school in London with a three-year course in the technique that has influenced countless actors, musicians and others in the decades since. At the heart of Alexander's technique is a belief in reducing tension in the neck and so freeing it from compressing the spine and thus allowing freedom in and lengthening of the back. It is the upright position of the spine that makes us erect and a free spine allows us to balance and stay upright with the minimum of effort.

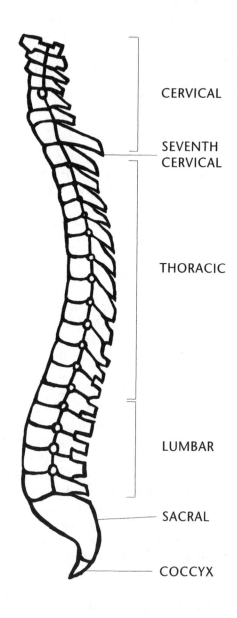

CERVICAL

SEVENTH
CERVICAL

THORACIC

LUMBAR

SACRAL

COCCYX

The Spine

This workshop teaches the actor what the spine is, how it is constructed and how it works. It is an intimate workshop requiring close physical contact between participants. Ideally, it should be done in pairs but in an odd-numbered group one or more teams can be of three.

Our backbone keeps us upright. It is the conduit for all the nerves in our body. It is made up of thirty-three bones called vertebrae. The row of lumps down the back are called the spinal processes.

Find a partner.

· Have them bend their head forward. The prominent vertebra at the base of the neck is the seventh. Use it as a reference point to find the others.

The six above it disappear into the skull. The first vertebra, at the very top inside the skull, like the god who held up the world, is called the atlas. Like the seventh, the first is one of the seven cervical vertebrae. Below the cervical vertebrae come the twelve thoracic vertebrae.

As you travel down the spine you will feel the bones becoming larger. As they become larger so they become more capable of movement.

Below the thoracic are the five lumbar vertebrae, the biggest and the most capable of movement. There is an abrupt change from the less mobile thoracic vertebrae to the more mobile lumber vertebrae. Here, in the area of the eleventh and twelfth, is the commonest place to break one's back. Below the lumbar are the five fused bones that make up the sacrum – the Latin for 'sacred'. No one knows why the sacrum is so named, but it relates closely to the base chakra, one of the energy centres of the body that we will look at in Chapter Seventeen.

At the bottom of the sacrum is the coccyx, so called because of its supposed resemblance to the beak of a cuckoo. This is made up of four or five very small vertebrae that are joined in humans but are the movable base of the tail in some animals.

Feel the bones. Feel them being felt. Find as many as you can feel. Swap over.

This will be unfamiliar to most actors and although the exercise is best done in silence, there should also be plenty of opportunity given to discussion between partners at the end of each part of the workshop, sharing experiences and feelings. With a large enough group you can also try this in a circle with each person working on the back of the person in front of them, building vertebra by vertebra in synchronicity as we did with the foot massage.

> Stay with your partner.
>
> Stand beside your partner and stand on your two feet. Distribute your weight. Be comfortable. Be balanced.
>
> Hang forward like a puppet whose strings have been cut.
>
> A single thread suspends you from your sacrum.
>
> Your partner is going to assemble your spine and bring you upright by massaging each bone at a time.
>
> Slowly uncurl – don't stand up straight but uncurl your spine.
>
> Your partner should massage the bones already uncurled at regular intervals.
>
> Slowly, gently, you will uncurl until you are fully upright.

This is very difficult to do. We are not used to thinking of using our back as a series of individual bones but tend rather to think of it as a single entity, hinged at the waist. Educating the body to use every joint, every muscle and every bone is crucial to all the workshops in this section. It is only by understanding and feeling how they work that they can be applied in the infinitely different ways that may be required in performance.

> Your head should be loose.
>
> Your partner should gently swing it every so often.
>
> Let your partner do all the work.
>
> Relax.
>
> Swap over.

Different cultures have different relationships with the vertical, and centre themselves at different points. This profoundly affects their acting traditions. The Alexander technique makes much use of the chair and of sitting and standing in easy, efficient ways. Alexander was part of a Western acting tradition, upright and led by the head where the seventh vertebra is a key to movement.

> Repeat the exercise but in reverse.
>
> Stand upright.
>
> Find your partner's seventh vertebra, the most prominent at the back of the neck. Curl their head down from there working your fingers gently into their skull.
>
> Then curl them down from the seventh all the way to the coccyx, massaging as you go.

One aid to precision in this is to use small adhesive stickers to mark the vertebrae as you go. Use mirrors if you have them. Performers can see their own spines in a mirrored room and so do not have to work in pairs. They can run their fingers up and down their own spines and explore themselves.

> Supporting your partner and paying close attention to the seventh and lumbar vertebrae, help them to sit cross-legged on the floor.

Eastern and Southern cultures have a closer relationship with the floor than Western cultures do. They make less use of the chair and when they do, it becomes a symbol of power, status and authority rather than a utility for comfort. I have an African chair carved for a tribal leader from a single trunk of wood. Sitting on it is very different from sitting on a Western chair. One is close to the ground, yet thrust forward by the carving at its back, poised ready for action.

In Asia, sitting on the floor is often preferred to sitting on chairs. This leads to a different physicality in the Eastern performer to the Western performer, characterised by a different centre of gravity. This relationship to the ground is a crucial difference between Western/Northern performing traditions and Eastern/Southern traditions. Firstly, the body sits closer to the floor in Eastern/Southern cultures; secondly, the bare foot is placed on the bare floor. Finally, there is stamping and the making of noise with the foot while the hand movements are delicately articulated. All these aspects of performance make for a very different use of the body and its relationship with the performance space. These differences will be explored throughout the book. This relationship to the floor can be seen at its most extreme in the Japanese movement form of butoh. The form is characterised by white-painted bodies, contorted postures and movements that are slow almost to the point of stillness. We are at a point of stillness now and will move our bodies even closer to the floor.

> Your partner sits cross-legged on the floor. Curl and uncurl their spine from the sacrum to the skull and back again.
>
> When they are curled tightly and comfortably, roll them gently on to their side, foetus-like.

We have finished where the next workshop begins. But this is a workshop that bears repetition and it is one that I often return to with my actors, to release tension, to counter bad habits and to reawaken an awareness of how this most important part of the body works. The spine not only keeps us vertical; it is also the conduit for all our nerves, transmitting our thoughts between our mind and our body, controlling all of our motion and activity. It is only through this understanding of the way in which the body works, and how it works efficiently, that an actor can know how to apply it to the creation of a character or the making of a performance. The way in which a character uses their spine can be key to realising them on stage. You only have to think of Richard III to realise how a crooked back can affect thought, motion and activity, or of John and Winston in *The Island* by Athol Fugard, bent from years of back-breaking work, repetitively moving filling and emptying their wheelbarrows. Think of Hamlet's spine lengthening when he tells us he will be very proud, revengeful and ambitious; Prospero's spine losing the strength of his magical powers as he breaks his staff; Winnie's spine growing out of the sand in Beckett's *Happy Days*.

Chapter Four

STEPPING INTO SPACE

James Weldan Johnson, in his version of 'The Creation', has an image of God walking the world into existence:

> And God stepped out on space,
> And He looked around and said:
> I'm lonely –
> I'll make me a world.

From the moment our ancestor *Homo erectus* stood upright and began walking with purpose into the unknown, human beings have peopled the landscape, creating the world as they have travelled. Our first movement workshop will begin with that first walk into the unknown.

Find a space in the room.

Let your weight pour into the floor.

Monitor yourself.

Here it can be useful to revise some of the exercises from the previous workshops and talk through the foot, the spine and the standing work. The necessity for constant reminders should always be borne in mind. The idea of being centred, relaxed, balanced and neutral is crucial to this workshop. Every time that we return to this centred neutrality, take care that everyone in the group has really made the return, monitoring them as the workshop proceeds. This is magic neutrality, the point of everything and nothing, which ensures that the character of the performer does not leak into the character being performed.

Is your weight more to the right or to the left?

Which foot is taking the more weight?

Having worked hard to establish and maintain balance with the least possible effort, we are now going to use the perfection of that balance and a shifting of it to create movement.

Fall a little off balance.

Make subtle shifts in your weight.

Think back to the detail of your feet; feel your balance shift; feel the effects in the rest of your joints as the weight shifts.

Now we are going to start to move.

Push into your toes. What happens?

Push into the side of your left foot. What happens?

Follow this push through till your body is propelled. This is one impulse. Stop when the energy runs out. Return to neutral. Then push again.

Relax.

This relaxation is central to the exercise. Everything should be done with only the minimum of effort. The slightest shift of weight or muscular impulse should be enough to effect a result.

It is important that each movement is the result of only one impulse. When the energy of that impulse is used up, exhausted, the body will come to a rest. Just a bend of the knee or a wave of the wrist should be enough to send the body into action. Our body is mostly water. More than 70 per cent is fluid. The slightest movement will ripple through the whole body. Time should now be spent experimenting with different starting impulses and different degrees of energy. It might be necessary to suggest impulsive movements. Downward sideways movements are often the best to start with – a shift of the hip, knee or ankle, say, or a thrusting of the buttocks. Play and experiment but for now have participants working solo. Much of this activity is similar in style to contact improvisation, the influential choreographic form developed by the American choreographer Steve Paxton in the 1970s. As its name implies, contact improvisation is about physical contact being the catalyst for spontaneous dance, and while it can be danced solo or in groups, contact improvisation is most usually seen in duets, in which the sharing, swapping and exchange of energies is the impetus for the dance.

IMPROVISATION

Now we improvise.

Using the energy of just one impulse, travel in the space.

As the energy is expended, come again to a point of stillness.

From wherever you have stopped, find another impulse and travel again.

Push into the floor and follow the impulse through.

And again. *Really* push into the floor.

As this happens, remember the foot that is making all this possible and the ground, which it pushes against, reacts to and always returns to. All movement is a use of gravity, harnessing it to make travel possible. Gravity holds us to the ground but it is our sense of balance and our manipulation of balance through movement that keeps us upright and makes travel possible. So far we have been working individually, but now we are going to begin to work as a group. Slowly we are beginning to build an ensemble of performers.

Push into your toes.

Follow the movement through.

Push into your right heel.

Follow this push through till your body is propelled. Stop when the energy runs out. Return to neutral. Then push again.

Relax. Monitor yourself. Be balanced. Be neutral.

Now move again, from whatever impulse you choose.

This time, become aware of the other bodies moving around you.

If you come to another body, meet it.

Your movements may block each other, or you may find that they combine and you are moving together. Either of you may then start the next movement.

Their impulse may set you moving. Your impulse may set them moving. You may both move together, synchronised, or apart.

Relax. Become neutral and balanced. Monitor yourself.

It is important to always return to neutral and not to let the physical memory of the exercise influence the exercise that follows. The Nigerian choreographer Segun Adefila shouts 'Shake it off! Shake it off!' at points of transition in a workshop and this is a useful way of executing a transition or finishing an exercise. Always allow time for balance, centring and the re-achievement of neutrality.

Now is the time to repeat the exercise. If you have enough participants divide into two groups so that each can watch the other. Again, the importance of observation, of oneself, of one's partner and of the wider group, should always be remembered and used as a tool by the workshop leader. After a while, when everyone is relaxed, confident and imaginative about what it is they are doing, you can add some music, the lines of song which can accompany the impulse to move across the landscape of the room.

Work with everyone having a space in the room to start from. The music can be used to create impulses to start movements. These may be individual or a number of people may be inspired by the same moment.

Increase the interaction between the bodies. You are allowed to block each other physically just by stopping where you do.

We are adding in rules here as we go, but as with all these exercises, simplicity is the key. The fewer the rules the less the performer has to hold in their head and the greater the opportunity for creativity.

Keep using the floor.

Keep using your feet. Everything that happens must come from there.

If you become tired or begin to lose concentration, step out.

Allow time for discussion whenever you think it appropriate. With some groups there may be little need or use of discussion in the exercise, but with another group, or with some individuals within the group, it may be very useful. Much will depend on how much physical work they have done before. Now to end the workshop we will bring everything together and create a short improvised performance.

Start with an empty space.

Position yourself somewhere on the edge of the space.

Your impulse will take you into the space and it may also take you out.

When you are in the space you are performing.

When you are out of it you are observing but ready to perform.

Listen for the music.

Choose a piece of music that is long enough for the size and energy of the group. Five to ten minutes might be enough but you can risk going for longer. The space can be empty at any point or full of all the participants or any variation between. If you are working on a text, choose music that is appropriate to the mood, atmosphere, environment or culture that you are exploring or creating. For Theatre Nomad's production of Shakespeare's *Pericles* we used the music of Raï to explore sounds, rhythms and cultures of the North African world of the play.

You've created a performance.

Chapter Five

THEATRICAL SPACE

The *Natya Shastra*, the Hindu holy book, written two hundred years before Christ, tells us that for the gods the size of the theatre is beyond limit but for mere humans a theatre should be no bigger than sixty-four *hastras* long and thirty-two *hastras* wide. One *hastra* is the length from the tips of the fingers to the elbow, the biblical cubit that God used when He gave instruction to Noah for the building of his ark.

This next series of workshops is about the exploration of stage space and the ways in which performers both define the space in which they perform and place themselves within it. They are about the self-disciplining of the performers' bodies, the ways in which they move and the ways in which they relate to each other.

For this exercise, the whole room, to the walls and into every corner, will be our working space. If you are the workshop leader, you will be in the space as you direct the workshop, like Tadeusz Kantor, the Polish artist and director, who would direct his plays from within, among the actors, even when they were being performed in front of an audience.

SHAPES IN SPACE

Walk in the room.

When you hear a shape called out, form yourselves, as a group, into that shape.

Work in complete silence.

Cooperate with each other. Be precise.

A square.

A circle.

A triangle.

Then combinations:

A circle and a triangle.

A square inside a circle.

The combinations and variations are endless. Spend time on the precision of this. A circle is an easy and familiar shape to make but a perfect circle is something else. Be aware of the creation of the shapes among the group but also of the placing of the shapes by the group in relation to the rest of the room. A circle should be in the exact middle of the room unless you choose to place it somewhere else. The corners of a triangle or a square should be clear corners; the opposite sides of an oblong should be of equal length. Individually and collectively your performers should be conscious of the space they are performing in and their ability to fill it. Even with three, two or just one actor it is possible to do this exercise. Ensure that no one dominates the group. Break up any domineering dynamic with a sudden change of object, from one square, say, to ten circles or twelve triangles and a square.

Once you have achieved geometric precision with simple shapes it is possible to move on to more complex, less easily defined shapes. A star is a good one because it can have any number of points. You may find that the group creates its star flat on the floor or standing in three dimensions. If the performers decide to put in little movements, their stars may even twinkle. If you call for four or five stars, they may all be different. Always return to walking in the space between shapes, to reclaim the entire room. Having used the precision and discipline of geometry to fill the space, you can then, through the freedom given by the stars, move on to the creation of concepts. Again with the group working collectively and in silence, create the universe in the workshop room. Use the opportunity to let your performers' imaginations fly. Throw out the challenge and let them explore what is possible.

If you are working on a text, this is a good moment to move to the specifics of the play. So you might want to create Illyria, the Forest of Arden, the Cherry Orchard, Prospero's island or John and Winston's island, Bluebeard's Castle or Bartholomew Fair.

Per Edstrom, the Swedish theatre designer and architect, has a theory that all the theatres in the world are developed from a few simple, basic forms which have been created by the shape of the borderline which the actors put between themselves and their audience. The origin of all these most basic forms can itself be found in the way in which a crowd moves so as to place itself around any real-life event.

The decision as to how you lay out the space in your workshop room will affect the eventual audience outcome if there is to be one. For the moment we are working in a situation where the workshop participants are also the observers. Edstrom has said that 'people form themselves into a circle when they want to discuss something so important that they all must have an equal opportunity to act and speak'. So it is that the circle becomes the natural shape for the making of a workshop space within the room. A workshop is a circular world.

This next exercise reacts against the natural pull of the circle and helps create a discipline within the actor to use the workshop space to its fullest potential.

THE GRID

Find a space in the room.

Imagine that there is a grid painted on the floor.

You can only move on the grid.

Straight lines one way.

Straight lines the other way.

You can only turn at right angles.

Begin walking.

Establish the grid.

Halve the speed you are walking at.

A gentle walk.

Define the grid clearly as you walk.

This is surprisingly difficult to do. Some actors I have worked with have simply never been able to fully achieve this simple discipline. A grid is a sequence of squares and of squares within squares. So within the room there should begin to form an infinity of straight lines, of right angles and of squares. It is worth spending time establishing this grid with real precision. An actor who can make this work understands the stage space they are in and its infinite possibilities.

Some members of the group may need real help in achieving this, but do not stop until you feel everyone is doing the work to the best of their ability. Allow time out for the participants to watch each other. Once things are going well, play with the size of the squares and with the speed of movement. Make the right angles really tight. We are moving between real and imagined space and the imagined will only have a reality if the details are secure.

The grid is a constant point of reference for many of these workshops. We will return to it again and again. I first came across it working with the director and musician David Baird and have used it constantly ever since in workshops we have led together and in ones I have led on my own. It is a wonderful and simple device. It ensures that the space is used to the full; is a common starting point for all of the group; gives a structure to move away from or return to; allows for much variety. You can dictate the sizes of the squares or not, the speed of movement, introduce cross-patterns – diagonals, chessboard moves. Above all, it creates a discipline in the group of performers and a collective dynamic.

End the workshop by playing with the size of the performance space and its placement in the room. Use the *hastra* or cubit as your measurement. Remember the injunction of the gods that you must not create a theatre that is bigger than sixty-four *hastras* by thirty-two.

Chapter Six

THE JOURNEY OF LIFE

Life is a journey. We spend the first half of our lives discovering our bodies and what they can do; having discovered all they are capable of, we spend the second half of our lives watching these abilities diminish. Most of what we learn about our bodies, and the skills we develop to use them, we learn in the first few months and years. When we are first born our primal need is for sleep. Soon our senses and motor skills develop. We can recognise a human face and our mother's voice almost from the moment we are born. We learn to hold things, to sit up and to crawl. By the time we are a year old we are beginning to walk and to say the simplest of words. This workshop returns us to those early months and then takes us on to the journey of life.

LEARNING TO WALK

Find a space in the room.

Lie on the floor.

Imagine, for a moment, that you are in the womb.

The human body is 70 per cent water.

You are a fluid within a fluid. You are floating in the womb. Supported.

The fluid content of the body always comes as a surprise. Even those parts we think of as being the driest of our body, our bones, are 30 per cent or more water. Water is never still. On those rare moments when you might think that it is still, the slightest disturbance can make movement apparent. So it should be with the human body, and many of these exercises work with the idea of fluidity of human motion being but the slightest impulse away. The unborn child does nothing for itself. It does not breathe. It is part of an environment far, far removed from the one we inhabit in the rehearsal room. From the moment it leaves the womb, the

newborn child must learn about the world that it can now sense
and be a part of.

> Imagine, for a moment, that you are a child asleep. You've never
> walked before.
>
> When you wake up you are going to find a way of standing upright
> for the first time.
>
> Having stood upright you are going to teach yourself to walk.
>
> Remember the floor.
>
> Feel the pull of gravity.
>
> Find balance, a way of using your limbs and joints.
>
> Become more confident.

This is a wonderful exercise to watch and a liberating exercise to
be a part of. Performers will easily give themselves up to the task
of learning to walk and, with these few instructions spoken quietly
and slowly, will open their eyes into the room having unlearned
all that the early months of their lives taught them. Some
performers will work entirely on their own in this exercise. Others
will cooperate with each other. Some will laugh at the misfortune
of others. Others will aid the slower learners. As with all these
exercises you can add in or take away rules as you like. The
performer may be aware of other performers or kept in their own
space.

> When you are walking confidently, when it requires no special
> effort, relax and experiment. Try different ways of walking.
> Embellish with speed and direction. Explore the world around you.
> Everything is new. Play.

All performance involves a journey. So does any workshop. In
some of these exercises the journey is explicit, clear, with a
destination in sight. In others the journey is concealed, implicit;
the destination may be unclear or of multiple possibilities – these
are often the most exciting journeys to be on. The journey that we
all have in common is that from life to death, and it is an
interesting one to explore in the workshop room. It can be used in
the creation of character, in the exploration of character, and in

the understanding of the body and its relation to age and experience. The body changes; its occupation of space changes; senses change; relationships change. Here is a very basic Birth to Death exercise that can be varied in any number of ways. You can start with the Learning to Walk exercise and move from there, or you can start from this point.

BIRTH TO DEATH

Find a space in the room.

You are two years old and have just learned to walk.

Explore the room.

You are five years old and it is your first day at school.

Your first day at high school.

You are sixteen.

You are eighteen and starting university.

Leaving university and starting your first job.

Twenty-five.

Thirty.

Forty.

Maybe you're married.

Or just best friends.

Fifty.

Sixty and maybe retiring.

Seventy.

Eighty and in an old people's home.

Along the corridor to bed.

Death.

These instructions are just indicators. You might have different ones, or want to be much more precise if you are building characters or exploring texts. It is easy to do this decade by decade, but the age and experience of the performer will make a great difference. The young performer will find it easy to differentiate between sixteen and eighteen, but not between, say, fifty and seventy. I have done this exercise with performers in their twenties who have become decrepit when they have reached fifty, an unnerving sight when you are a fifty-year-old running the workshop. The experienced performer should be able to act any age, absorbing the physical detail of the ageing process, whether it is becoming older or younger, into their own neutral body.

Work on the detail – go from, say, forty to fifty year by year, even season by season and month by month: you are forty and it is spring; forty-two and it is summer, and so on. Play with relationships, of lovers, colleagues, family and friends, transient or for life. Lives will intersect. People will die and new people will come in and out of the lives that are being lived in the workshop. Like a round in a song not everyone has to be at the same point at the same time. This is a linear exercise but with work it should be possible to join the line at any point. It should also be possible to work in reverse, to start old and become young. The exercise can then be applied to character and the journey of characters acted through the stages of their lives. An actor playing a part can pick up their character at any point on that character's journey, and often acting is about the intersection of two journeys, that of the actor themselves and that of the character they are playing.

We often ask how old a character is. How old is Hamlet? But age is a relative thing. If you are rehearsing *Hamlet* use this exercise to explore the relative ages and lives of all the characters. Perhaps Polonius is the oldest. Send your Polonius actor on his journey from birth. At what point are the other characters born and when do their lives intersect? Gertrude could be a mature woman or a teenage bride when Hamlet begins his journey. Where will Claudius be? At what point does Hamlet meet Horatio? Perhaps Yorick, reduced to a skull in the play, can be a living body in the workshop. Fill your empty space with the journeys of your characters' lives.

Chapter Seven

THEATRE OF THE GODS

The great Hindu teacher, the guru Bharata Muni, tells the story of the creation of drama in the *Natya Shastra* by the Supreme Being who invented drama. At the request of the other gods, Brahma, creator of the universe, extracted the four elements of speech, song, mime and sentiment from the four books of the Knowledge of Life. And so a fifth Book of Knowledge was created and the gods performed the first play in Heaven. Bharata details and codifies every form of dance, mime and drama and gives rules for everything, from the building of theatres to costumes, make-up and acting. The book is written for the playwright, the director and the actor: the three people essential to the creation of *nataka* which in Sanskrit means both drama and dance – a theatre that can make visible on stage the eternal moral and spiritual truths. Bharata writes of drama being not just for pleasure but as the exhibition of *bhava* (cosmic expression), 'to create wisdom in the ignorant, learning in scholars, afford sport to kings, and endurance to the sorrow-stricken; it is replete with the diverse moods, informed with varying passions of the soul, and linked to the deeds of mankind – the best, the middling and the low – affording excellent counsel, pastime and all else.'

Using a compass, mark out north, south, east and west on the walls or floor of the room.

THE GLOBE

Find your space.

Lie comfortably on the floor with your feet pointing east.

Raise your knees and place your feet on the floor.

Ground yourself.

Monitor your body.

You are lying on a globe. The surface of the globe is moving eastwards. At a thousand miles an hour.

Close your eyes. You are travelling with the surface of the globe at a thousand miles an hour.

Slowly roll on to your side and then stand up. Do this quietly and gently, being aware all the time of the globe you are travelling on.

Feel your feet on the ground.

Work up through your body.

Monitor your stance and your balance.

You are standing on a globe. The globe is moving eastwards. Face east.

Close your eyes. You are moving ahead. You are moving at a thousand miles an hour.

Maintain your balance as you travel at that speed.

Monitor yourself and be sure you are centred.

The gravity of the globe you are standing on is pulling you, holding you to the ground.

Your feet are on the globe. Eight thousand miles beneath them are another pair of feet.

Feel that connection.

Feel that movement.

Feel the molten heat in the centre of the earth.

Feel grounded.

Remembering the work we did on the feet, and the building of your spine, let the energy move through your body. Starting with your feet.

Be ready to move.

This exercise is a way of giving your performers a feeling of the importance of gravity. Gravity is the force that roots us to the ground. We constantly use our sense of balance around our own centres of gravity to stop ourselves from falling over. Shifting that balance, however minutely, sets our bodies into motion. Perfect balance around our own centres of gravity is what makes us centred, neutral and ready to perform.

Eugenio Barba has developed a theory of the suspension of an actor's energy ready for action. He believes that 'energy can be suspended in immobility in motion'. For Barba this is the moment when action is about to happen, a moment of tension, the cusp between preparedness and motion. Barba calls this 'sats', a moment of supreme poise, of 'dynamic preparation'. For Barba, as for Hamlet, 'the readiness is all'.

TABLEAUX VIVANTS

Stand towards the edge of the room facing the centre.

Anyone can go into the space and strike a pose.

Anyone can join them.

Come and go.

One person can be in the space.

Or the entire group.

Spend time observing as well as taking part.

This is the simplest of exercises yet can have the profoundest of performance outcomes. There are infinite possibilities as to what you will see. Many of the outcomes will anticipate work you will do in subsequent workshops. Images will appear, develop and dissolve; characters will form, interact and reform; strands of narrative will come into existence. You may see one performer huddle on the ground; another may come in and hug them; others may join and pull them apart or extend abstractly from this central core. Religious imagery will often make an appearance: blessings, prayer, crucifixion. The cycle of life may begin and end and begin again with birth, ageing and death. Be prepared to witness anything and have the courage to allow the work to continue until it comes to its own resolution. This might be a space empty of performers or a space full of everyone, or an image so compelling that no one wants to disturb it. If you are leading this workshop, the instructions should be kept as simple as possible. As with most of the exercises in this book, the simplicity, clarity and brevity of instruction is often the key to getting the best of results. This exercise has a number of uses but for the moment we are using it in three ways:

- As a way of putting the body into motion
- As a way of giving the performer an awareness of the impetus to go from stillness to movement and back to stillness again
- As a way of beginning to work physically with fellow performers

What will be created is a series of interlinked, constantly shifting tableaux. Depending on the group this might become a continually moving piece with only one or two members static at any one time. The piece should always be about the containment of energy and the preparedness to move again. Remind the group of Hamlet's injunction that the readiness really is all. A lot of physical contact is involved in this work and it can be a very good way of breaking down inhibitions in a group of actors new to each other.

Repeat the exercise with music. Many of the workshops in the book benefit from the use of music and the choice is crucial. I always travel with a case of CDs ready for every eventuality and some have been used time and time again. Your own taste is important but two guiding thoughts have always been useful to me in my choice of music. One is the importance of rhythm and repetition, which is why the American minimalists are regular companions. I find John Adams to be one of the best companions of all. He uses the metaphor of travelling through landscape to describe his music. He writes of how in his music 'a *paysage* of one distant terrain comes into view and then slowly gives way to a different vista'. That resonates with many of my images of the actor being a traveller in a created landscape. The second thought is about the number of players in the music you are using. Never let the performers of the music outnumber the performers in your space without good reason. It is important that what is being created by your performers is of a similar scale to what is being played by the musicians whose performance you are borrowing. Above all, it should be music with a pulse. The ideal would be to create the music yourselves like the gamelan orchestras of South-East Asia where the musicians intensely watch the actors who themselves listen to the musicians, the two groups working in perfect harmony. So, return to the previous exercise but this time with music.

TABLEAUX WITH MUSIC

Stand towards the edge of the room facing the centre.

Listen for the music.

Anyone can go into the space and strike a pose.

Anyone can join them.

Come and go.

Listen for the music.

One person can be in the space.

Or the entire group.

Spend time observing as well as taking part.

Let the music be the beginning and the end.

You have created a performance.

This is a wonderful exercise both for a group coming together for the first time and one that has worked together for many years. It is extremely simple, and the less the rules are elaborated, the further it can go. The choice of music makes a big contribution and can help if you are using this workshop for the exploration of a theme or a text. This can be abstract or it can be culturally, historically or geographically specific. What you create can even become the building blocks of a performance piece. You can add objects, which might also be used to explore themes and imagery within a text. When the nomads performed the story of Faustus we used a crucifix in this exercise. The God in our production was a wonderful Brazilian transvestite, Lulu Macumba, for whom the crucifix became a tool in his game with Mephistopheles.

Chapter Eight

LIFE GAMES

The making of theatre is the creation of order out of chaos. The running of a workshop is a perfect illustration of chaos theory. The best-known example of chaos theory is that of the butterfly effect. In 1960, the meteorologist Edward Lorenz was experimenting with the problems of predicting the weather when he realised that the tiniest of events in one part of the world can affect the weather thousands of miles away in another part of the world. The flapping of the wings of a single butterfly in Japan can cause a tornado in Indonesia or a hurricane in Florida. Similarly, the beat of the wings of another butterfly can stop something happening that otherwise might have happened. There was nothing original about the butterfly effect but what was original was its application to a whole new field of scientific thinking. The flutter of the butterfly's wing is the impetus for transformation. The smallest variation in the initial conditions can result in unforeseeable and potentially enormous transformations, leading to major and unpredictable outcomes.

Much of this physical work is about the creation of patterns in the space of the workshop room and is related to the playing of games. Chaos theory explores the way in which order creates itself from chaos and the way in which patterns emerge from the apparently random. One way in which it manifests itself is in John Conway's 'Game of Life'. Like these workshops, Conway's is a game with no winners and losers. Once the pieces of the game are in their starting places, the rules of the game determine everything that happens later. Conway devised his game to explore ideas of emergent complexity and self-organising systems. Basically this is a field of science that explores how highly complex patterns and modes of behaviour can emerge from the simplest of rules. At its heart it seeks to explain how the beauty, complexity and diversity of everything we see around us can have developed from the simplest of starting points.

Conway's 'Game of Life' was originally played on a board.

Today it is played throughout the world on highly sophisticated computer systems. There is no reason that it could not be played with a large group of actors on a huge playing field. With a few 'cells' on the chequer board of the game, our workshop grid, all moving to a few simple rules, hugely complex groupings and systems of cells develop and take on a 'life' of their own as the game progresses.

This workshop, like some of the others, plays with ideas of theatrical creation similar to Conway's ideas of scientific creation and also relates to the ancient playground game of follow-my-leader.

The workshop can have a number of starting points. They could be stories told among the group; skills, memories, or characters from a script that you are working on. It is important that they are individual to each group member. Everyone in the workshop should start with a different impetus from everyone else. Let us use personal skills as an example.

FINDING THE ESSENCE OF AN ACTIVITY

Find a space.

Think about something you enjoy doing. It can be a hobby or a sport. It must be something you know well. It is often best if the activity is something that is not performance-related, so no dancing or singing or martial arts but rather knitting or horse riding or gardening or reading, etc.

In your space act out your activity.

Spend time getting the detail right.

Every movement of the body enables you to do what you are doing.

Remember all our other workshops and feel the detail of all that you are doing.

It is one of the wonders of running workshops that from exactly the same starting points entirely different results may occur. The differences will be down to the equivalent of the fluttering of the butterfly's wings in the room, the stimuli that are given to the group. Much of that will be under your control as workshop leader, but an infinity of other fluttering butterflies may be in the room, over which you have little or no control. Sometimes it helps to do this work in pairs, to enable observation and questioning of what it is that is being done.

Find a partner.

Demonstrate your activity to them.

Have them replicate your activity and then you replicate theirs.

Explore the essentials of what it is that you are doing.

Try and get to the core of the activity through the use of your body.

Emphasise the important actions and abandon the unimportant.

Gradually reduce your activity to its bare physical essentials.

Use your partner to help decide what works best and what is clearest and easiest to observe and understand.

Have your partner show you your own activity and show your partner theirs.

Now it is time to show all that is being done to the rest of the group but with each participant demonstrating their partner's activity, not their own. Discuss what has been shown. How easy is it to recognise the activity from the essential movements it has been reduced to? Encourage simplicity and clarity of movement and encourage the use of the entire body. No part of the body is uninvolved in any physical activity, however passive that activity might seem at first. This is not mime. It transcends mere mimicry and is about getting to the essence of a physical activity, stripping away the inessential and getting to the heart of what makes an activity active. It is about using the minimum of effort to recreate an activity theatrically and make it true. It is about the way in which an activity inhabits and affects the entire body. Even something as apparently inactive as reading a book will involve the whole body; the movements of the eyes, the turning of the page with the hands will set up a reactive chain through all 'dem bones'.

ESSENCE OF A FEELING

Return to working individually. This time we are going to work not with an activity but with a feeling.

> Find your space.
>
> Remember a moment of fear.

I am using fear as an example, but it could be a moment of happiness, of despair, of elation or anything else. You might choose an emotion or a memory that is relevant your text or your exploration.

> Something that happened to you.
>
> Walk and remember that moment.
>
> Let it inhabit your body.
>
> Build this systematically, from the feet through the whole body, reusing some of the previous workshops.
>
> Monitor your movements.
>
> Make the movements more extreme.
>
> What are the keys?
>
> Where is the movement led from?
>
> How is it balanced?
>
> How does the breath work?
>
> What are its characteristics?
>
> Spend time distilling the movement into a few components.
>
> Keep searching for the essence.
>
> Distil further into three distinct moves that can be repeated.
>
> Refine to clarity.
>
> Put in a stop if you want to, or a pause.
>
> Transfer your movement to the grid.
>
> Once you are confident in what you are doing and in the clarity of your movements, take a chair and sit at one side of the room.
>
> When everyone is sitting in a line of chairs, take it in turns to show your movements.

Take a moment here to break and discuss. What works and what does not work and why? The choreographer Jane Turner said once that 'repetition is your friend'. And Athol Fugard talks of the 'controlled repetition' that makes performance.

FOLLOW-MY-LEADER

Each show your movements again.

As one person demonstrates, observe, and when you feel confident, follow. Change leaders.

Eventually, everyone will have copied each other's moves.

You now have a vocabulary of movement in the group.

Make another row of chairs at the opposite side of the room.

Sit in a line.

Play some music. Given that this is a workshop about the creation of patterns, patterning might be a factor in your choice of music.

When the music starts, anyone can get up and do their movements on the grid.

Anyone can follow.

Anyone can break away and start their own movements or join someone else's.

Everyone can be doing their own movements; everyone can be following one movement; or any combination.

At any time you can sit out and observe.

You can make as many or as few rules as you like and there are infinite variations. As always with these workshops, and as chaos theory and Conway's 'Game of Life' tell us, the least and simplest of rules can have the greatest and most unexpected of results. The bodies of the performers become the 'strange attractors' of quantum physics. Patterns are being created on the floor of the room, shapes are being made in the space of the stage, order is being formed from chaos, just as life forms itself in Conway's game.

Stop when the music stops.

You've created a performance.

This workshop is an ideal exploration of character.

CHARACTERISTIC MOVEMENTS

Choose a character from a play you know well, perhaps a text you are working on.

Choose an activity or a feeling for your character.

Let your character inhabit your body. Begin to move.

Explore your character's movement and begin to move it to an extreme.

What are the keys?

Where is the movement led from?

How is it balanced?

How does the breath work?

What are its characteristics?

Spend time distilling the movement into a few components.

Keep searching for the essence.

Distil further into three distinct moves that can be repeated.

Refine to clarity.

Put in a stop if you want to, or a pause.

Transfer your movement to the grid.

You can continue with the follow-my-leader variation. This not only helps your actors explore their own characters by observing their physicality when it is taken up by their fellow actors; but it also enables all of your actors to have an understanding of the physicality of all the characters in their collective performance.

On the grid of the workshop floor you have, like Conway on his infinitely large conceptual computer grid, begun to create life, an infinitely variable theatrical world.

It is time to start speaking.

BREATH

'And the Lord God formed man of the dust of the ground, and breathed into his nostrils the breath of life; and man became a living soul.' The words from Genesis echo those of the Ugandan proverb that says that 'life is your ability to breathe in every time you breathe out'. In the fifty years between my birth and writing this book I may have taken some four billion breaths. Most of them, unless I have been overexerting myself, or having a lesson in Alexander technique, or rehearsing a troublesome song, I will not have noticed. We breathe in as we enter this world and we breathe out as we leave it. Our breaths are what mark us as being alive. To breathe in is inspiration; to breathe out is expiration. To breathe is to be inspired.

INSPIRATION

Find your space.

Lie on your back.

It is important to be comfortable and it is important to be in close, relaxed and fluid relation to the ground. It is useful to remember previous workshops about the foot and the back. The knees should be raised and the feet planted firmly on the ground. Remember everything we did with the feet in the very first workshop. Revise that in detail if need be. As the workshop continues, monitor the actors, just as they should constantly be encouraged to monitor themselves. Shift feet and heads if necessary, use hands on the ribcage and shoulders to increase your actors' consciousness of what it is they are doing.

Close your eyes and relax.

Become conscious of your breathing.

Breathe in.

Breathe out.

Breathe in.

As you draw breath in through your nose, the nose warms and purifies the air.

Through your throat and into your chest.

Breathe out.

From your chest.

Through your throat and out through your mouth.

Nose, throat, chest.

Chest, throat, mouth.

Breathing was the first thing you did as you entered this world and it will be the last thing you do as you leave it.

As you breathe in and out of your chest, feel the spine behind, lying on the floor.

Feel your ribs curving from the spine around to your breastbone.

Breathe in.

Breathe out.

At the floor of your chest, separating it from your abdomen, is your diaphragm – a large muscle.

Breathe in.

Breathe out

For most of us, the diaphragm is a mystery that is difficult to comprehend. It is a muscle that divides our body in two and it is the muscle that, with the help of the ribs, opens our lungs. We will examine its working more closely in the next workshop, but for now just imagine various parts of our breathing system as we refer to them.

Inside your chest are your lungs – cone-shaped containers of air. Just as your ribs are smallest at the top and largest at the bottom, so too are your lungs.

Breathe in – inspire. Think about that word.

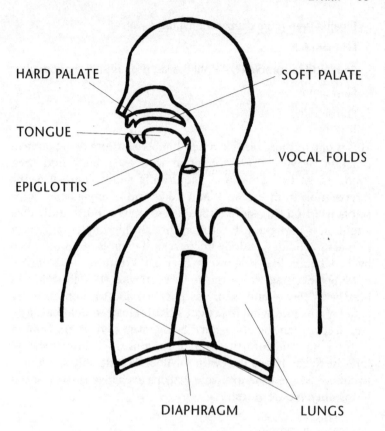

HARD PALATE

SOFT PALATE

TONGUE

VOCAL FOLDS

EPIGLOTTIS

DIAPHRAGM   LUNGS

Lungs and diaphragm

The lungs are passive. It is what surrounds them that makes them breathe. The lungs are elastic so will spring closed when released by the ribs and diaphragm.

Breathe out – expire.

As you inspire, the cavity of your chest is enlarged. You contract and flatten the abdomen. You raise the ribs and expand them sideways. You raise the shoulder bones and collarbones.

Breathe in.

Breathe out.

Your lungs are rarely used to their full capacity.

Breathe even more deeply and fill them with air.

Fill them full.

Empty them completely – until the last drop of stale air goes out.

New air in.

Old air out.

This is one of those rare exercises that benefit from being done in isolation, leaving the actor alone with their body and their thoughts. At the same time, monitoring and occasional gentle intervention from the workshop leader can be invaluable. Some actors will find this more difficult than others and so individual attention is important. Breathing, though the simplest and most primal of activities, is done unconsciously and is often inhibited by bad habits like shallow or irregular breathing and breath-holding. Encourage the actors to listen to what they are doing, to breathe as slowly and gently as possible, and to monitor every detail of this most vital of activities. Each breath should be bigger and deeper than the one before, being taken right to the bottom of the lungs and into the back of the ribs. Each breath should increase the body's contact with the floor. We use only about one-twentieth of the total available gaseous exchange surface of our lungs when we are at rest.

Breathe in – inspire.

Breathe out – expire.

As you breathe in, take the breath right through your body.

Feel your ribs, shoulders and spine move.

With each breath feel the movement pass through your body.

Slowly allow the breaths to become bigger.

The air you take in is coming from ever further away.

The air you breathe out is coming from ever deeper inside the alveoli of your lungs.

The alveoli are the tiny air sacs inside the lungs where the oxygen is absorbed from the air you breathe. They can expand to an amazing degree, every square centimetre of alveoli can expand to no less than 300 square centimetres of tissue surface. And inside our lungs are 300 million alveoli.

Breathe in.

Fill 300 million alveoli with air.

Let the 300 million alveoli take the oxygen from the air you breathe.

Breathe out. From 300 million alveoli.

Breathe in.

Be inspired.

Breathe out.

Feel the movement of your breath move through your limbs.

Through your lungs and legs into your feet.

With each breath, feel your feet pushed more firmly into contact with the floor.

Feel your arms extend and your hands open.

Breathe in.

Breathe out.

Grow as you breathe.

Breathing gives life and allows the actor to create life. It is part of the cycle of creation.

Breathe in – inspire.

Breathe out – expire.

Imagine the breath bringing life into your body.

Imagine the air you breathe in coming from the furthest corners of the atmosphere and being taken down into the bowels of the earth.

Breathe in.

Breathe out.

As the breath comes deep into your lungs, the life-giving oxygen is extracted from it and carbon dioxide is breathed out in exchange.

Breathe in.

Breathe out.

The carbon dioxide you breathe out is taken in by the plants around you which themselves give off oxygen in return.

Think of yourself as part of that eternal cycle.

Breathe in.

Breathe out.

To get a sense of the power of the breath and of the moving lungs, try this:

THE POWER OF BREATH

Face the wall.

Breathe in.

Use your out-breath to propel yourself backwards into the space.

Use your in-breath to suck you back towards the wall.

Breathe in and out.

Move to and fro.

Forwards and backwards.

How far can you move in each direction?

Your in-breath makes you light, it inspires you and gives you the power to move.

Control the release of your ribs and diaphragm and so control your movement with your breath.

Next, move to controlling the breathing among the group and develop an ensemble of breath power. You can work in one large group or a number of smaller groups.

One person stands in the centre of the room.

That person closes their eyes.

Breathe deeply.

Breathe yourself as light as a balloon.

Everyone else in the group stands around the one in the centre.

Now, ever so gently, because they are as light as the air inside of them, blow them around the room.

Everyone takes it in turns to be blown and so feel the power of their breath and the lightness that breathing can induce in the body. Having experienced the power of even the gentlest blowing breath, have everyone find their own space in the room.

FIRST SOUNDS

Breathe in.

Through your nose, warming and purifying.

Down your windpipe.

Into your lungs.

Breathe out.

From your lungs.

Through your windpipe.

Through your larynx – your voice box.

Into your mouth.

Over your tongue.

Under your soft, then your hard palates.

Through your teeth.

Feel it pass your lips.

Repeat the cycle again.

This is a slow and gentle exercise and should not be rushed. Through the course of the workshop the participants will get ever more familiar with the mechanics of their breathing and the rhythm of their breath of life. Allow plenty of time for this familiarity to grow. Breathing is about repetition. The constant repetition of our breathing is what keeps us alive. Let your actors repeat each part of the workshop as often as they need to develop an ease and depth to their breathing and sound-making.

It can be useful to do this exercise sitting, either cross-legged on the floor or else in a chair. In this position it becomes easier to pull the breath right down into the body, down to the bottom as if the breath were opening the anus and making contact with the base chakra at the bottom of the coccyx. This is one of the energy centres we will explore in Workshop Seventeen.

> Now you are ready to make sounds.
>
> As you breathe out, your larynx is going to transform that breath into a sound.
>
> As your breath moves through your larynx, start with the smallest sound possible.
>
> A whispered 'ah'.
>
> On each out-breath let it grow almost imperceptibly.
>
> Each out-breath is making a louder sound.
>
> Slow, steady breaths.
>
> Hear the sound move away from your body as it leaves your lips.
>
> Listen to it travel into the air and into the atmosphere until you can hear it no more.
>
> Let the sound grow with as little effort as possible.
>
> Feel the resonance in your mouth, your nose, your face, your cheeks, your sinuses, your head.
>
> You are filling the room, and beyond, with sound.
>
> And when you have made the biggest sound possible, begin to make the sounds quieter. Until you return to silent breathing.

It was with a group of actors in the capital of the Czech Republic that I recreated one of the great legends of Judaism and one of the archetypal stories of all cultures, the creation of human life by man. In the city of Prague, so legend has it, the Rabbi Judah Löw ben Bezulel breathed life into a humanoid creature, a golem that he had made from clay. And it was there, many centuries later, in the shadows of the old Jewish cemetery, that four actors breathed life once more into an old story. The golem, like Frankenstein's monster, wreaked havoc wherever he went and destroyed the rabbi and the rabbi's beautiful daughter. As the rabbi found to his cost in the Jewish quarter of the ancient city of Prague, only God can truly breathe life into His creations. So strong was the fear of going against the word of God by the man-made creation of life, that acting itself was banned under the laws of the Christian world from the time of Christ until the Council of Vierre in 1311. This inaugurated the Feast of Corpus Christi and allowed, for the first time, the performance of liturgical plays by the laity. To act is to breathe life into a creature that is not you; it is to make, as the early Christian fathers believed, a new living soul. Of the millions of breaths that they have between entering this world and leaving it, an actor will give many millions of them to the creation of lives other than their own. To act is an awesome thing.

Chapter Ten

A WORD OR TWO

Dancers usually prefer not to speak and to keep the use of their mouths for cigarettes and celery. Jane Turner asked me one day to come and work with her company of dancers. The piece they were working on required the dancers to speak. To the dancers this seemed an insuperable obstacle. The important thing, I thought, was not to be afraid of the text. Take it one word at a time. And that is what we did, starting with the simplest of words, each with a single syllable. The words 'yes' and 'no'. But before we even got to the words, we thought about our breathing.

Having worked mostly individually in the last workshop, this one is one best done collectively: in pairs, in threes or even with all the participants working as a single group. The instructions are written for pair work but can easily be adapted. We are going to explore the way we breathe in more detail and begin to make more sounds and eventually real words.

As we found out in the previous workshop, our lungs are supported by our diaphragms and surrounded by our ribs. Our ribs make a cage or basket that hangs from our spine. As we expand our ribcage so our lungs expand with it.

FINDING YOUR RIBS

Find a partner.

You are going to help each other to breathe.

One of you goes first.

Stand easily in the room.

Support yourself on the floor.

Find your balance, centre yourself and be neutral.

Become aware of your breathing.

Breathe into your ribs and into your back.

Your partner is going to hold your ribs and help you breathe in and out.

Try to keep your stomach still as your ribcage expands.

Let your diaphragm expand the bottom of your ribcage.

Let your ribs open your lungs.

There are twenty-four ribs, paired twelve on each side of the body.

Feel for them and count them or have them counted.

The curves of the ribs become more open the further they are down the body. The first seven pairs are attached directly to the sternum or breastbone. Sternum comes from the Latin word *sternere*, which means 'to spread', and you can feel the strong bone spreading your ribs out from your heart. These seven pairs of ribs are called true ribs. Below the true ribs are the eighth, ninth and tenth pairs, the false ribs, which do not join the sternum directly but are connected to the seventh rib by cartilage. Below these are the eleventh and twelfth pairs, the floating ribs, which are half the size of the others and do not reach around to the front of the body.

Find your partner's sternum.

Counting from the neck down, find their ribs.

The first seven, the 'true' ribs, attached to the breastbone.

The next three ribs, the false ribs, attached to the seventh.

Finally the last two, the 'floating' ribs.

Monitor the breathing as you feel the ribs.

Feel them move as they expand the lungs.

Breathe gently in and out.

Once you have discovered all of the ribs, hold them or have them held as you breathe.

Breathe more deeply with every breath.

The monitoring hands should move out further with every breath as you breathe more deeply.

Your stomach should be as still as possible.

Only your ribcage and your diaphragm should be moving.

And with them your lungs.

We only use 20 per cent of our lung capacity during normal breathing. The lungs are elastic. We need the muscles of our ribcage and diaphragm to expand our lungs, but like anything made of elastic they will return to rest of their own accord.

Breathe gently and deeply.

As you breathe, you are filling yourself with air.

Making yourself lighter.

Breathe into your back and into your seventh vertebra.

You are breathing yourself up into the world, lengthening and relaxing your spine as you go.

Every breath in is an inspiration.

When you are ready, relax and swap over.

You can now go on to work as a group.

With one person at the centre of the group, the rest are going to help that person breathe and help them understand and monitor their breathing.

Some can hold the stomach and the back, others the ribcage.

One should monitor the seventh vertebra.

All should guide the breathing of the person in the centre and feel for every change that happens.

Everyone should have a chance to be the focus of this work. Spend time until each person in the group has been monitored and monitored everyone else. When all have had their chance and talked about what has been discovered, have everyone find a space and lie on the floor.

Breathe.

Remember the feeling of all those hands on your body.

Breathe slowly, steadily and deeply.

Listen for the other breaths in the room.

Gradually bring your breaths together.

Unison breathing.

Nothing should be spoken.

Now it is time to make some sounds.

Float a whispered 'ah' on the out-breath and remember the cycle of breathing from the previous workshop.

Bring all you have learned in the workshop into your breathing.

Listen to those around you.

Bring your breathing together.

Let the volume increase until you fill the space and beyond.

Make the sound only on every third breath so you can hear it float away.

Listen before you begin to say a word.

Make sure breathing is perfect before you start to put words on it. It is time at last for some words. The words are 'yes' and 'no'. There are no simpler words. In learning any language these are the ones to start with. They are clear in their meaning. We all know what 'yes' means and we all know what 'no' means. This is a moment to explore how much variety in the sound, emotion and intention can be conveyed in the way in which we speak the words we use. It is also a moment to have some fun after so much physiology and quietness.

THE YES/NO GAME

One person sits on a chair in the middle of the room.

They can only say the word 'no'.

Everyone else is on the periphery of the space.

They can only say the word 'yes'.

The person in the chair is the most desirable creature in the whole wide world.

Everyone else wants to be the person they go off with at the end of the workshop.

Start when you are ready.

That should be all you need to say. Things will probably start quite gently and quietly with whispered, cooed 'yeses' from across the room, or furtive 'yeses' in the ears of the seated participant. Soon there will be every variety of vocal expression, great energy and not a little madness. Even dancers will be speaking with intensity, passion, commitment, desire, aggression, delicacy, beauty, hope, despair, disappointment and much else besides. So much will be found in two little words. Encourage your performers to use all they have learned about the apparatus of breathing and making sounds to explore every possible way of expressing variety with these two simple, single-syllable words. End it when you want to, before mayhem or debauchery breaks out, unless the workshop ends itself when the seated one themselves suddenly uses the 'yes' word. You can add in an extra chair at some point, sit someone on it and announce that another person, equally or even more attractive, is in the room. The dynamic will begin to shift and the exercise may end, as it has done for me, with the two seated performers saying 'yes' to each other.

Chapter Eleven

BLIND MAN'S BUFF

Children have been playing blind man's buff since before drama began. It was played by the ancient Greeks and is found in every culture. For the Germans it is blind cow, *Blinderkuh*, for the Spanish blind hen, *gallina ciega*, and for the Italians blind fly, *mosca cieca*. When adults played it in rougher times, the blindfolded player was hit, 'buffed' as they used to say, often with a stick. This workshop uses the gentler version of the game and is about developing listening skills as a performer by listening for the breaths of fellow performers.

You will need a volunteer. There is nothing worse than the uncertainty and unease that can be generated by asking for a volunteer in a workshop. It is important, in a group who have done little work together, that you instil complete confidence among the participants in what is happening and in your ability to run the workshop. So be in control of events at all times. Sometimes one person may be particularly keen to do an activity, but that may not always be apparent. It is one of your jobs as the workshop leader to constantly watch out for nervousness and insecurity, to support the nervous and insecure members of the group and to moderate overenthusiasm or excessive ego in other group members. With most of the workshops in this book, the training element is such that everyone should do the activity at some point. But there will be some workshops when lack of time will dictate that only a few can experience everything while others watch. A gambit I often use is to ask for a volunteer and then, if there is no immediate response, to choose one: 'We need a volunteer . . . and it's going to be *you*.'

Blindfold the volunteer.

Disorientate them by revolving them and moving them in the space.

Everyone else find a space, ensuring that the group is spread pretty evenly around the room.

Breathe with a whispered 'ah' on the out-breath.

Start quietly, gradually increasing the volume until the room is full of audible whispered 'ahs'.

The blindfolded player now has to locate all the other players by listening for the sound of their breath. As each player is found, they should move to the edge of the room and return to silent breathing. When the last person is found the blindfold can be removed and that last person is then blindfolded. So the game is repeated until everyone has had his or her turn.

It may be possible for the blindfolded player to recognise individuals by the sound of their whispered 'ahs' and this can be used as a variation so that the game continues until everyone is correctly recognised. Another variation is for participants to make their own individual sound instead of a whispered 'ah'. And the players can be allowed to move in the space. With each new blindfolded player add in a new variation.

One variation is 'blind man's staff'. The blind man carries a stick while the rest of the group walks around him in a circle close enough for the stick to reach them. When the blind man points with his stick, whomever it points to has to grab hold of it. The blind man asks, 'Who's there?' and the person holding the stick has to whisper, 'It's me,' and be identified by their voice. If they are recognised, they then take over as the blind man.

A baby is able to recognise its mother's voice before it recognises anything else in its new-found world. Newly-born animals can find their way back to their mothers often over vast distances just by following the sound of their voice. We lose that acuity of listening as we grow older. This exercise helps us to relearn it.

RECOGNISING VOICES

Find a partner.

Listen to the sound of their whispered 'ah'.

Let them listen to yours.

Listen hard until you are confident that you can recognise your partner's sound.

Then all the participants are blindfolded and led to different places in the room, keeping partners far apart from each other.

Using only the sound of your whispered 'ahs', find your partner.

Again, there are a number of possible variations. You can do the exercise as a blindfold race with half the group at one end of the room calling to their partners at the other end with their whispered 'ahs'. You can work with half of the group at a time so that the others can observe. You can change the sounds of the whispered 'ahs' to animal sounds. You can use words or even text. You might be Oberons calling your gentle Pucks to 'come hither', or Prosperos telling your Ariels to 'approach . . . come'. You might be Lady Macbeths calling on the 'spirits that tend on mortal thoughts', or Joan La Pucelle's calling on 'charming spells and periapts'. Whatever you decide, allow time, as always, for observation and for listening from outside of the exercise. Finish by swapping partners and using a variety of sounds and words until the air is full of whispers. Then let your actors find each other in pairs or groups until, as everyone is found, the sounds die away and only the sound of silence remains.

Chapter Twelve

A SHAKESPEARE SUMMER

London, 1605. Shakespeare had never seen a Japanese person before, so he was intrigued by the group of eleven sailors queuing for a place in the pit for that day's performance of The Tempest. *He did not recognise their exotic clothing and strained to understand something of the sharp and quickly spoken language with which they were conversing. He listened intently but could not understand a word. The Irish builders repairing the theatre box office were easier to understand, but then he had been used to hearing the sound of their language since he first moved to London. The crowd of Africans were jabbering in another tongue he could not understand. The spectacle of the capoeira Angola, the Africans kick-fighting for money with knives tied to their ankles, distracted him for a moment or two before he hurried into the theatre with some rewrites for Richard Burbage who was playing the magician in his new play. Throughout his walk from his digs to the Globe he had not heard one word of English.*

As the play started, the large crowd listened intently, hanging on every word even if they understood only a fraction of what was being said. Many of the phrases, even individual words, were new to them, coinages of London's most successful playwright. All the more reason to listen with care to the play they had come to hear. What was it that the strange foreign creature in the play was saying about language? Something about it being only useful to curse with? That they understood.

As this imagined scene based on what we know of Shakespeare's London shows, its population was diverse and polyglot, 'so rich an assembly of countrymen and foreigners' that the west door of St Paul's Cathedral was littered with notes from language teachers and translators for the Arabs, Turks and Russians who were doing business in the city. Now they would need Japanese translators too. Perhaps one in ten of the teeming population were from overseas. This was the diverse and multilingual world in which Shakespeare wrote his plays and in which he created the English language, as we know it. In the babel of voices that was Elizabethan London, people trained themselves to listen and to understand in order to survive on the streets and to enjoy the plays that brought them together in the theatres of the south bank of the river.

Nowadays we go to see plays rather than to hear them. That is if we go to the theatre at all. More likely we watch films and television. Our eyes have taken over from our ears as the prime receptors of dramatic information. So these first workshops on the voice are as much about learning to listen as they are about learning to speak.

We will start listening and speaking in this workshop with just a two-word phrase. The phrase is 'summer's day' and it comes from a sonnet by Shakespeare. First, we need to read the whole sonnet, become familiar with it and learn the first two lines.

SONNET 18

Shall I compare thee to a summer's day?
Thou art more lovely and more temperate:
Rough winds do shake the darling buds of May,
And summer's lease hath all too short a date:
Sometime too hot the eye of heaven shines,
And often is his gold complexion dimm'd;
And every fair from fair sometime declines,
By chance, or nature's changing course, untrimm'd;
But thy eternal summer shall not fade,
Nor lose possession of that fair thou owest;
Nor shall Death brag thou wander'st in his shade,
When in eternal lines to time thou growest;
　　So long as men can breathe, or eyes can see,
　　So long lives this, and this gives life to thee.

Give some time for the sonnet to become familiar. Participants should find a comfortable space to read the sonnet to themselves, playing with it quietly on their tongue, feeling it in their mouth and face. When you sense that everyone is ready, bring the group together in a circle that is as big as the room can take. The bigger the room the better. No space is too big. I have never done this workshop on a football pitch, but one day, if I get a chance, I will.

Don't speak.

Make eye contact across the room and find a partner.

Silently decide between you who will speak first.

Whisper the first two lines of the sonnet across the room.

Almost inaudibly.

As quietly as you can.

And as clearly as you can.

Listen to the lines being said to you.

Your partner listens to the lines being said to them.

Try and pick out every word.

Listen for phrasing and colour.

Receive the thoughts being sent to you.

Gently repeat the words, concentrating on everything you are saying.

Never rise above a whisper.

Swap over and repeat the exercise.

When you are ready, relax, join your partner and discuss what you have done.

This opportunity for discussion during a workshop is important. Sometimes it is best done privately, other times you might want to bring the group together for a more formal sharing of thoughts and experiences. Now it is time to work on just our two-word phrase, 'summer's day'. Each participant should find a quiet and comfortable space in the room where they can be alone with their thoughts.

Think of the best summer's day you have ever had.

Remember it through all your senses.

How did it feel, taste, smell, look, sound?

Remember the details of time and place.

Who were you with?

How old were you?

What was so special about the day?

What made it summer for you?

That is probably as much instruction as you need. Leave plenty of time for thought and memory. Introduce each trigger (sense, time, place and so on) gradually. Each one should lead to clear and detailed memories. When you have a sense that everyone is ready you can begin a game of tag using just the first line of the sonnet. Choose a person to start.

Make eye contact with someone else in the room.

Hold all your thoughts and memories in your head and body about your special summer's day.

Say the first line of the sonnet.

Say the line just once or as many times as you need.

Use the word 'summer' to travel you across the room.

Try and convey eveything about that summer's day in the way you speak and move on the single word.

Physicalise the word as you move.

Listen as your partner moves towards you.

Hear everything that is being communicated to you in that one word.

Suit the word to the action and the action to the word.

Observe everything you are being told by the way your partner moves.

The first receiver of the line then makes eye contact with another member of the group and transmits their version of the line, imbued with their special summer's day. Eventually, everyone will have spoken and travelled with the line and the room will be full of summer days. Each recipient should say something about what they heard and try and describe the summer's day that was brought to them. Then the performer of the line should recall the day themselves. Now a number of variations are possible. Perhaps just one of the many summers is chosen by the group and all try to convey it through physicality, movement and the use of just the one line until the whole room is filled with one memorable summer's day.

One of my most memorable summer days was in a place called Klipplaart, a remote little town in the African Karoo. This is dry and barren land where the rusting hulk of an old steam train is the only testament to the industry which once gave this town a purpose. The trains do not stop here any more and the few who still find employment in the town somehow make a living from the land. There is a huge breeze-block community hall which is used as a theatre of sorts and it was there with the nomads that we were entertained with gumboot dancing, a cappella singing and a devised play about the evils of the demon drink. We were the only white faces in an audience of maybe two hundred black Africans for whom Xhosa and Afrikaans were the languages of daily communication and English was virtually non-existent. We had to listen hard to a performance in languages we did not understand, concentrating on and responding to every nuance of speech for clues. After the performance given for us, it was our chance to perform in return. The audience wanted to see our little group of European players act Shakespeare in English. We had no set with us; we had no costumes or make-up; we were without our props. We were just actors with words that few would know. But inspired by the performance that had just been given for us we performed for them. Our story, I said through the Xhosa transla-tion of the poet Looks Matoto, was of two princesses, an evil duke and a contest between a professional fighter and an unknown stranger. I pulled back the makeshift curtain and the wrestling scene from *As You Like It*, which in our production used capoeira Angola instead of wrestling, began. Few, if any, of the words were understood by an audience who had never left this small town, never met Europeans, certainly never seen Shakespeare. Yet every nuance was understood. The revelation for us, the heresy even, was that somehow Shakespeare could transcend language. The power and simplicity of his storytelling, coupled with actors determined to convey the narrative and bring alive their characters, gave – for perhaps ten or fifteen minutes – the clearest, most powerful, vibrant performance of Shakespeare I have ever seen. The flirting between Rosalind and Orlando, the friendship between Rosalind and Celia, the aggression between the fighters, the realisation of Orlando's love for Rosalind – no moment, no nuance went unnoticed by an audience who hung on every look, glance and word even if they had not heard it spoken before, and felt no embarrassment about reacting loudly and enthusiastically to everything they saw and heard. I felt privileged to be there, 'at the end of the world' as the mayor called it when he thanked us afterwards, watching actors from five European countries performing words written four hundred years ago on the other side of the planet and, by the thought and detail of their acting, putting across all that the words could mean.

Chapter Thirteen

TEXT

Now that we have an understanding of how the breathing and the vocal apparatus work, and have spoken and listened to a few words, we can move on to text. As with all the work on the voice, this is a workshop as much about listening as it is about speaking. It is about using the hearing apparatus as well as the speaking apparatus and it is about the importance of speaking and listening as physical activities. You will need some text. This could be from a play you are working on or the workshop participants could choose individual speeches. You could use some of the pieces of text in this book – the sonnet, or the lyrics of 'Dem Bones'.

Choose a piece of text.

Lie on the ground. Feet on the floor.

Breathe and become aware of your breathing.

Breathe into your back and set up the cycle of breath we worked on in the previous workshop.

Read the text to yourself, silently, in your head.

Now read it quietly to yourself.

Breathe and read.

Read and breathe.

Now read the text silently again, listening to your breath as you do so.

We are beginning to attach words to breathing and breathing to words. Time can be spent moving back and forward with this exercise, vocalising sometimes and reading silently at others. Reading is a physical activity even when we are not reading aloud. This exercise takes us to the root of the words by trying to internalise the thoughts before speaking.

READING ALOUD

Keep the thoughts of the words of your text but express them only as thoughts and breath.

With the words in your head you are going to recite the text with your breath.

Find a partner.

Find a space.

Choose your text.

Lie on your back.

Have your partner put their head on your chest.

Read the text to them, but firstly silently in your head. Do not say the words out loud.

Pay attention to your breathing.

Speak the text with your breath.

Slowly add the words out loud on to the breath.

As quietly as possible let the words be heard.

If your head is on the speaker's chest, listen to the breath and listen to the words.

Repeat but a little louder.

Then say the text once more but silently, on the breath.

Relax and discuss in your pairs what you have experienced.

Talk about the text, the words, the thoughts and the breathing that went with it.

It may be that after discussion you want to try other things out. Allow the participants to come up with new ideas or try things in different ways. If necessary, repeat some of the breathing work from earlier workshops.

When you are ready, swap over and repeat the exercise.

This exercise is about listening, about concentration and about the importance of breath in communicating thoughts and words. There are a number of options here which can be used to change or add focus. Experiment with where the head is placed. It could be on the partner's chest or their stomach or any part of their vocal apparatus. The text could be whispered in the ear. Participants can experiment with working back to back or face to face. Eyes can be open or closed. What helps with hearing and with concentration? Is it just the mouth, like that in Beckett's *Not I*, that is important to the auditor?

> With your partner find a comfortable place in the room.
>
> Lie or sit on the floor, whatever is most comfortable.
>
> Relax.
>
> Have your partner read their chosen text to you.
>
> In a whisper but with all the intensity of feeling that is possible.
>
> Swap over and do the same again.
>
> Now sit back to back.
>
> Feel that connection.
>
> Breathe into your back and into your partner's.
>
> Spend time just listening to and feeling each other's breathing.
>
> Establish a shared cycle of breathing.
>
> Read your texts to each other.
>
> Listen for any key words.
>
> Repeat, but echo the words in your partner's text that are key to you.
>
> Discuss.
>
> Then swap over and do the same with the other text.

We can now begin to transfer the communication skills that are being developed, from an intimate personal space into a public one while at the same time maintaining all the intimacy.

> Now make as much space between you as possible.
>
> Have the whole of the workshop space between you.
>
> Breathe and think the text.
>
> Then, with all the concentration and intensity you can, read your texts to each other. From right across the room.

Communicate from the greatest distance that the room allows but with the lowest volume of voice.

We will finish with dialogue, sharing one piece of text between two performers, bringing breathing, speaking and listening together over the whole workshop space.

With your partner choose one piece of text.

Share the text between you.

Perhaps alternate lines if it is a poem.

Stand closely back to back.

Establish a rhythm of breathing together.

Breathe deeply into the small of each other's back.

Begin to speak the text.

Maintain the breathing.

Listen.

Speak.

Gradually move away from each other as you repeat the text.

Create patterns as you move and fill the space with traces of your voices and your bodies.

Finish by hearing all of the texts that have been chosen, spoken by those who have chosen them.

Walk on the grid.

Break away from the grid when you begin speaking your text with your partner.

Return to the grid when you have finished.

Anyone can start.

You have brought voice and body, speaking and space together.

Chapter Fourteen

RHYTHM

As we continue to bring together the body, the breath and the voice, we will need to find rhythmic texts to work with. Rhythm is important because it implies movement. There are some good verses in this book, from 'Dem Bones' to Sonnet 18. You can use those for these exercises but should begin to build up a collection of your own. Your performers should also build up their own portfolios of material. You might explore other sonnets; we will use one as an example in this workshop. You might find other metrical verse. Children's nursery rhymes are a rich source of material. Here is one to use for the first exercise in this workshop.

> Oranges and lemons,
> Say the bells of St Clement's.
> You owe me five farthings,
> Say the bells of St Martin's.
> When will you pay me?
> Say the bells of Old Bailey.
> When I grow rich,
> Say the bells of Shoreditch.
> When will that be?
> Say the bells of Stepney.
> I'm sure I don't know,
> Says the Great Bell of Bow.

Find a partner.

Moving their hands around, your partner holds your ribs, your stomach and your neck as you breathe.

Establish the breathing and an even, rhythmic cycle.

Begin to speak the verse as your breathing is supported and monitored by your partner.

Just the first line.

Be silent on the in-breath.

Use the whole of the out-breath for the line of verse.

Each line is a breath.

Be inspired on the in-breath for the thought that you speak on the out-breath.

Practise until you can do this with ease.

Then add in the other lines until you can speak the whole verse, one line to every out-breath.

Remember the 300 million alveoli that are exchanging the oxygen in the air we are breathing in for the carbon dioxide we are breathing out. We talk today of the exercise that increases the efficiency of our body's intake of oxygen as aerobics. It was an American doctor, Kenneth H. Cooper, who pioneered the idea of aerobic exercise and his book *Aerobics*, published in 1968, has been so influential that we now take the idea of aerobic exercise for granted. Cooper's aerobics stimulate both breathing and heart rate long enough to cause beneficial changes in the body. Much of the physical activity in these workshops is inherently aerobic and many of the exercises can be developed to increase aerobic activity. As your performers work on their breathing they will stimulate their hearts and a stimulated heart is a great muscle for a performer to have.

This work should be continued until it becomes effortless. This may take many workshops and can be returned to again and again over subsequent workshops until breathing and speaking are in perfect harmony.

Swap over with your partner and repeat the exercise the other way around.

Repeat again, this time finding different voices for the different bells in the verse.

Now you can add in some movements with the speaking of the text, but at first without moving from the spot. The soft relaxed movements of t'ai chi ch'uan are ideal. The aim should be to have breathing, voice and bodily movement all working together as one, in harmony.

T'ai chi translates as 'the great ultimate'. It is first mentioned in the *I Ching*, the Chinese Book of Changes, as the union of yang (active) and yin (passive) from which all else flows. T'ai chi ch'uan is 'the great ultimate fist' and a martial art, but internalised and not used for combat. Its free-flowing, rhythmic movements are exercises to harmonise the yin and the yang of the practitioner. The principles of t'ai chi have been practised for centuries, perhaps as early as the third century in China. Today, across East and South-East Asia, public parks are full at dawn and dusk with people following their master in the ritual exercises of t'ai chi to start and finish their days. When I have been running workshops in Hong Kong or observing them in Phnom Penh and Bangkok, the fact that such activity is built in to the everyday of the local population is itself an inspiration.

Fit the movements to the breath and to the line.

Think of your arm as a measurement of space, a *hastra* or cubit.

As you speak the line and move your arm, you are moving through space with the inaudible and noiseless foot of time.

Now we are ready to move the whole body through space and time. Choose another piece of rhythmic text, such as a nursery rhyme or a sonnet.

SONNET 27

Weary with toil, I haste me to my bed,
The dear repose for limbs with travel tir'd;
But then begins a journey in my head,
To work my mind, when body's work's expir'd:
For then my thoughts (from far where I abide)
Intend a zealous pilgrimage to thee,
And keep my drooping eyelids open wide,
Looking on darkness which the blind do see:
Save that my soul's imaginary sight
Presents thy shadow to my sightless view,
Which, like a jewel hung in ghastly night,
Makes black night beauteous, and her old face new.
   Lo, thus, by day my limbs, by night my mind
   For thee, and for myself, no quiet find.

It is useful to continue to work in pairs and make this a joint voyage of discovery.

WALKING AND TALKING

Breathe.

Speak the first line on the out-breath.

Weary with toil, I haste me to my bed.

Be inspired on the in-breath.

Think of the movement of the verse as movement of the body in space and walk as you speak a line.

Take paces, *hastras*, cubits, steps and movements of one foot in front of the other as you speak the line.

Weary with toil, I haste me to my bed.

Now the next line with the movement starting on the other foot.

The dear repose for limbs with travel tir'd.

Now, back on your starting foot, move to the third line.

But then begins a journey in my head.

Carry on for the fourth line.

Continue to move through the space on each spoken line.

Work through to the end of the sonnet.

Discuss your progress in every meaning of the word with your partner if you are working with one and then swap over with them and repeat the exercise.

Think of the beat of the verse that you use in the exercise as the beat of the heart, the vital sign of life. As we get older our heartbeat gets slower. For an infant the heart needs to beat at 120 per minute to sustain life. An adult heart beats at a much slower rate, just seventy beats per minute. This is useful to know as you adapt tempi to the situations and circumstances of these sonnets or to any verse. Try reading Jaques' 'Seven Ages of Man' speech from *As You Like It*, using that declining heartbeat as the measure of your performance.

A performer's voice works in three-dimensional space just as much as their body does. The three variables of body, space and voice make for a complexity of choices for the performer. An understanding of this can be developed with this basic exercise which can also function as a useful warm-up before a performance. Place four chairs in the corners of the room and choose a children's rhyme.

Choose a line or two of the rhyme.

Starting at any chair, speak the line.

Walk, as you speak, from one chair to the next.

Finish your walk and finish your line as you return to the chair at which you started.

The shorter the line you have chosen the greater the challenge of the exercise.

Vary the speed. Travel at a snail's pace or with the speed of a cheetah. Every time, the words should match the movements. The words and the performer should travel in the space at the same tempo, with the starting point and destination always controlling the action.

This next example of verse is a round. There are four lines so divide into groups of three or five so that as the verse is repeated a different voice has the first line.

> Frère Jacques, frère Jacques
> Dormez-vous, dormez-vous?
> Sonnez les matines, sonnez les matines,
> Din, dan, don, din, dan, don.

Stand in a circle.

One person says the first line.

The person to their left says the next line.

The person to their left says the third line.

The person to their left says the next line.

And so on, constantly repeating the verse.

Listen intently to the line coming before you.

Play with pitch, tempo and volume, but bring all your voices together so that you are using them as one single voice.

Keep this going at different tempi and dynamics until the rhythm becomes effortless. Whoever starts the line can make the changes. You can use accents, silly voices, and eventually put in movement, being led by a body part, say, so that the physical pattern and order in the room breaks down but the vocal pattern remains.

'Frère Jacques' is a round. As one person finishes the first two lines, the next can start with them and so on in potential endless overlapping repetition until the person who has started decides to finish and the other voices finish in their turn. End the workshop with the participants divided into four groups, performing the round all together. Start with each of your four groups in a different corner of the room. As they become more confident, all of them should move around the room, separating out and listening hard for their fellow group members across the space.

Chapter Fifteen

THE DRUM

In Africa the drums talk. They are used to communicate over vast distances, twenty miles or more. Talking drums are found in South-East Asia and Melanesia, but it is with West Africa that they are most associated. *Tambora* is the Xhosa word for drum, and the name taken by a group of young South African women performers with whom I have often worked. Talking drums are often referred to by the West African word *jembe*, or in its French spelling of *djembe*. The talking drum is characterised by the cords that run the length of the drum. Pulling or squeezing the cords changes the pitch of the drum in the same way that our vocal cords change the pitch of our human voice. The language of the drum is as understandable as spoken language in the cultures in which it is used. The drum is thought to imitate the human voice. Perhaps the human voice imitates the drum. Perhaps the two languages grew in tandem. For this workshop any drum will do. Even an inverted bucket or a biscuit tin will suffice if nothing else is to hand. The more sophisticated your drum, however, the more sophisticated will be the results of the workshop. To begin, it is important to become familiar with the use and sound of the drum.

> Someone take the drum and start a slow beat.
>
> The rest form a circle around the drummer.
>
> Walk to the beat of the drum.
>
> Let the drummer control the speed.
>
> Play with tempi.
>
> Make changes in tempi extreme.
>
> Improvise.

Let everyone have a chance to drum. If it is a small group this can be done now. In a larger group ensure that during the course of the workshop everyone has their turn. Find a line of verse, one you have used before or something new.

Form a circle around the drummer.

The drummer must establish a slow beat.

Walk to that beat, maintaining the circle.

Do not let the circle become any bigger or any smaller.

Begin to say the line.

Bring walk, drum and voice together.

Walk to the beat.

Beat to the walk.

Speak to the beat.

This is a simple start. Spend time establishing the regularity of beat, voice and step. The body and the voice should be as one. Remember and reinforce work from earlier workshops, especially the feet and spine and breathing.

Form a line and hold hands.

Drummer to one side.

Walk around the room in concentric circles, one person as the hub, turning on the spot.

Speak the lines again to the drumbeat.

Keep the rhythm.

Play with the speed.

Find a significant word and give that extra stress.

You are all moving at different speeds over different distances with different-sized steps, but keep breathing and voice together.

Someone now has to move, speak and drum all at the same time as we break the mood and energy with rhythm tag.

Work with a line from one of your verses.

Whoever is starting can choose the line used.

Find a space.

The drummer starts the rhythm and walks, jogs or even runs to it as they speak their line.

As they come up to others in the room they have to begin to move.

Keep going until all are speaking the lines as they move to the rhythm of the drum.

The drummer can change the pace at any time.

Make the line your own while still moving to the beat.

Play with the stress.

Emphasise the words that are significant to you.

The next part of the workshop should start gently after all that speed and movement. It is about intensity of listening, speaking, expression and understanding.

Pair up.

Find a drum.

Choose a text.

One partner is going to be the speaker, the other the drummer.

Sit on the floor facing each other around the drum.

Say the first line of your text.

Beat the rhythm of the next line.

Speak the third line.

Beat the rhythm of the fourth.

And so on until the end of the poem.

Do the same thing in reverse.

Beat the first line and speak the second.

And so on.

Now play with what you are doing.

Develop speaking, drumming and listening.

Play with rhythm, tempo, volume (with pitch if it is a proper speaking drum), meaning and rhyme.

Play with syncopation.

Develop what you are doing as a jazz improvisation.

Speak some lines, words or phrases and beat others.

Become free with each other as you say the same things in two languages: the language of drums and the language of voice.

This is a good moment to stop, share what has been done in the room, discuss and demonstrate.

Return to your pairs and put some distance between you.

Close enough for clear eye contact.

Speak the poem to each other again.

The whole poem spoken.

Then the whole poem drummed.

Gradually move apart from each other.

Increase the space as far as the room will allow.

Ignore the other drums and poems around you.

How far can you go and still be heard and understood?

This is a great workshop to do out of doors. Rehearsing *Macbeth* on the South African veld, our Lady Macbeth used a drum in the blazing heat of the day to call on the 'spirits that tend on mortal thoughts' to aid her in making her husband king. Our Lady Macbeth, Hannah Buvik, was Norwegian; our Macbeth, Jean Pagni, was French. Both were working in a second language, English. As we worked on the scene, the drum passed from one to another and it was as if a third language, the language of the *djembe*, had entered the scene as well. The drum became the voice of their thoughts as much as Shakespeare's language. In Africa the drums can communicate the subtlest of thoughts over huge distances. The actor's voice does not have the same power which is why the gods decreed that the size of a theatre should be such that there can be no more than sixty-four *hastras* between the performer and the auditor. As you listen to the drum and the voice, can you tell which is mimicking the other?

Chapter Sixteen

REVISION

We are halfway. It is time to recap and bring things together. Start with some revision, working briefly but methodically through the essential parts of all the previous workshops, building as you go. Some workshops will have been more useful to you than others. Some will have been more difficult than others. Some will still have unexplored potential.

Spend time reminding yourself and your participants about the way in which the foot is constructed and how it plants itself on the ground. Find that essential balance from which everything else will come. Work through the body and pay special attention to the spine. Revise the detail of what you have done before. It is the detail that easily gets lost. Remember all those vertebrae. Remember all those bones in the foot. Remember all the articulations in the body. Spend time on the hands. Go on a journey or two, on the grid and off it. Create patterns in the room. Play follow-my-leader.

Remember how to breathe. Have the members of the group find their inspiration as their breath enters their bodies. Have your participants hear themselves and each other. Fill the room with sounds and fill it with silences. Have every rib in the room felt by every hand. Play blind man's buff and recall some perfect summer days. Bring out the drum and walk and talk to the rhythm of its beat.

You have learned something about how your body works.

You have found out about your feet and about your hands.

You have discovered your spine.

You have explored the connections of the bones of your body and how you can articulate them.

You have learned to move your body by itself and in relation to others.

You have learned to move your body in theatrical space.

You have brought your body to life with your breathing.

You have attached voice to your breath and movement to your voice.

You have explored words and rhythm.

You have listened and been listened to.

You have travelled through space and time.

You have found your magic neutrality from which all performance is possible.

As you rework through the essence of the previous workshops you will have little epiphanies, revelations that you did not have before. Some workshop exercises will take on new significance in the light of ones that have followed them. All will be deepened and heightened as they are now seen as part of a developing programme of work. Allow yourself time to re-enjoy work that has gone before. Then, when you have touched on everything, shake it all off, have your performers find their own space in the room and come to balance. Let them stand comfortably in harmony with the floor, with their weight spread evenly into the moving globe they are standing on through their two feet. Monitor all your participants for their balance; monitor them for their breathing. When all are balanced, centred and at a point of magic neutrality, we will slowly throw them off balance with a word or two of text.

Think of a line or phrase of text. Something from one of the texts we have used before.

Begin to move gently around the room.

Maintain your balance, your centring and your neutrality.

Move easily and effortlessly.

Begin to speak the line easily and effortlessly.

Voice and body should be in harmony.

As you travel, imagine the voice originating from different parts of your body.

Start with the feet and the voice coming up through the floor.

Then into the groin.

Let this transformation happen slowly.

Shift the dynamics of the voice and body around and let yourself be taken off balance.

Pace and direction will change.

Now into your solar plexus.

Then your heart.

And on to your throat.

Your forehead is next.

Finally, as if from a golden thread, from the top of your head.

Shift between these centres at random. The voice will change, the sounds the body makes will change, as the focus of that voice shifts around the body. Change tempi. Shift gears quickly between one centre and another. Then slowly move the voice just by touching your performers on their bodies so that everyone is working differently and vocal and bodily discord breaks out in the group. Create chaos and then slowly re-establish order.

Bring the voice back down to the floor.

Up into your groin again.

To your solar plexus.

Your heart.

Your throat.

Your forehead.

Finally, as if from a golden thread, from the top of your head.

Walk lightly, carried by that golden thread.

Let the voice float away.

Breathe lightly and easily.

Find your own space in the room.

Bring your walking to a stop.

Centre yourself.

Be balanced.

Breathe deep into your body.

Reach a point of magic neutrality.

We are ready to move on to our hearts and souls.

Part Two

HEART AND SOUL

Introduction

The body and the voice are now ready for stimulation.

The second part of the programme is called 'Heart and Soul'. This is an eclectic series of workshops developing the performer's emotion, imagination and intuition. We work through senses and stimulation to find ways of creating character and performance. Then come workshops looking at ways of enabling the performer to control and tune their own performance. The book finishes with the use of all the skills developed over the whole programme in the creation of performance through narrative.

These workshops take us on a journey that includes sensual work, childhood games and disciplined movement. Body, mind, voice and spirit are all stimulated into action. Some of these workshops are collections of ideas, suggestions for activity – far less prescriptive than those in the first part of the programme. Creativity is balanced with ways of developing the performer's ability to control and discipline their performance.

The programme finishes with narrative and the telling of stories, applying everything that has been learned in all of the workshops to the opening up of the closed world of the workshop space to the demonstrated world of performance.

Chapter Seventeen

SENSES AND CHAKRAS

The workshop is a little like the children's game blind man's buff that we played before. Its purpose is to develop the senses, the sensory memory and the imagination and to heighten the use of senses other than sight. You will need blindfolds.

TOUCH

Find a blindfold.

Find a space.

Put on the blindfold and lie on your back, feet on the ground, knees raised.

Relax.

Breathe.

Explore the space using one sense at a time.

Feel the world around you. The floor underneath, the air around. Feel for the slightest movement in the air. The smallest particle of dust.

Our nerve endings are picking up stimuli. Our spinal cord is the conduit of those stimuli to the three pounds of weight that constitutes the brain and is also the conduit of stimuli back from the brain to the muscles. All this nervous tissue – nerves, spinal cord, brain – is the most watery part of our body. Eighty per cent of it is water. Everything we do is coordinated by this nervous sytem, stimulated by the inside of our body and the outside world around.

Slowly your performers will grow in confidence. Usually it is the hands that will touch first. The floor will be explored with the fingers and hands before the performer stands in the space. Even so, the urge to be upright will often become paramount and actors will be on their feet very quickly. Performers with other training, and this is especially true of dancers, will explore the space using all their body surface and their hands may not be the primary tools of exploration. Feet, buttocks and back can lead and a dancer will immediately work on different levels, close to the floor or reaching high into the air. I was made aware of this when the Hungarian dancer Andrea Molnär joined the nomads. As we began doing this workshop, Andrea used the three-dimensional space in a completely different way from the other performers, her shoulders, buttocks, the back of her head, exploring every corner of the space.

We think of there being five senses – touch, hearing, smell, taste and sight – and these are the ones we will use in this workshop. Scientists believe that there may be more than five, including two for sensitivity to pressure, two for sensitivity to temperature and one for pain. These extra senses are brought together into a single sense of touch. See if you can isolate them during this part of the workshop.

HEARING

Become still again and find a comfortable space.

Lie on your back, feet on the ground, knees raised.

Relax.

Breathe.

Hear the world around you. What is close, what is far away? Listen to the breathing of everyone else in the room. How many people can you hear? Who can you recognise? What faraway sounds can you hear? Build up a three-dimensional sound picture of the room you are in and the world beyond. Encourage listening beyond the confines of the room. It may be possible to hear distant traffic and the noise of planes or trains, to hear wind in the trees or rain on the windows. Listen for internal sounds. Can breath or blood or heartbeat be heard? Hearing is the sense that holds us to life. If we drift into unconciousness, it is the last sense to leave our body. If we awake from sleep, unconciousness or from coma, hearing is the sense which first reconnects us to the world.

Now allow the participants to move again.

SMELL AND TASTE

Smell the world around you. Smell yourself. Smell the scents in the air.

Perhaps you can *taste* as well. What tastes are in the air? What is in your mouth from breakfast, lunch, supper last night, your last lingering kiss . . .?

While taking the performers through this exercise, you can create a new environment around them that can be safely negotiated when blindfolded. Think of things they might hear, taste, smell and touch – perhaps salt on the floor, a quietly playing radio or two, or a scented cloth draped over a chair.

Gently roll on to your side, on to all fours, and slowly stand up.

Explore the room around you, using all your senses.

Allow plenty of time for this and take care to guide the performers if necessary. When people are beginning to tire, bring them back to sitting or lying comfortably in the room.

We have talked of five or more senses. Most cultures have a concept of a sixth sense, of an intuitive sensing of the world that is beyond the physical. Intuition is an important skill for an actor, perhaps more important than the merely physical skills which most actor training develops. Many of the workshops in this part of the programme are designed to stimulate and develop intuitive skills. This is a moment to concentrate on intuition as a sixth sense.

SENSE

Sense the room around you. What can you pick up beyond the senses that you have already used? What is the atmosphere in the room? What is the mood? Is there a history? Is there an energy to the room or coming from the group?

It is possible to perceive using all the senses at once. The word for this is *aisthesis*. Your performers will develop their *aisthetic* abililty using their five, six or more senses through these workshops. Some people confuse their senses and smell with their ears, taste with their eyes and so on. This is a condition known as synaesthesia. We still have one sense to go.

SIGHT

Take off your blindfolds.

What do you *see*?

Sight has been left until last because it can so easily dominate the other senses. Having experienced the space with the other senses your actor may see things that they had not noticed before.

Stop, sit, relax and discuss what you have experienced.

This exercise can be done in character. We used it with the nomad's *Pericles* to explore Pericles' recognition of his long-lost daughter through senses other than sight. You might concentrate on the importance of different senses to different characters in different theatrical situations – Lady Macbeth's razor-sharp hearing as she waits for her husband to murder Duncan, Gloucester's losing his eyes or Winnie's failing sight that clouds her 'happy days', the synaesthesia of the Ghost of Hamlet's father as he 'scents' the morning air.

We are now going to move through the body in a different way, basing our work on the chakras, the body's energy centres. This exercise can be used as an exploration of the performer's own body or as an aid to exploring the body of a created character. Chakras are the psychic-energy centres of the body. Today the concept is widespread in belief and healing systems in both East and West, but the theory of chakras has its origins in the occult physiological practices of Hinduism and Tantric Buddhism. Chakras are conceived of as focal points where psychic forces and bodily functions merge with and interact with one another. There are thought to be some 88,000 chakras in the human body but for most purposes, and certainly for the purpose of this workshop, we need think only of seven. Six major ones are located roughly along the spinal cord and another one is to be found just above the crown of the skull. These are the centres we used for moving the voice around the body in the previous section. Each of these seven major chakras is associated with a specific colour, shape, sense organ, natural element, deity and mantra (a monosyllabic repetitive formula for prayer). The most important of these are the lowest chakra (*muladhara*), located at the base of the spine, and the highest (*sahasrara*), at the top of the head. The muladhara encircles a mysterious divine potency (*kundalini*) that the individual attempts, through yoga, to raise from chakra to chakra until it reaches the *sahasrara* and self-illumination results.

Yoga is a Sanskrit word meaning 'union'. The original Indian philosophy of yoga dates from around 200 BC and is a spiritual progression towards *samadhi*, an ecstatic union with the ultimate reality. The physical stages of that progression, with their emphasis on physical posture and the development of breath control and a supple, flexible and healthy body, have become important in many performers' training, East and West.

For the performer, the important thing is to keep the energy channels clear and allow energy to flow through the body unimpeded. Working in this way allows bodily transformation to happen from the inside out, without the conscious imposition of stance, attitude and so on. It also allows one to find and constantly return to neutral.

CHAKRAS

Let your feet ground you.

Be centred and balanced.

Your feet are your connection to the world.

Feel the energy travel through your legs – equally on each side into the very base of your spine – into your testes or vagina.

This is your base or root chakra. It is around the sacrum – the sacred part of your spine. It is the source of your sexuality. It sets your physical boundaries.

Feel your own physical, personal space around you.

This is the chakra associated with your sense of smell.

Working on this chakra can immediately relate to the creation of character. Concentrating on this chakra will radically affect stance and personal space and so movement and relation to other people. With all of the other chakras, as we go through them, you

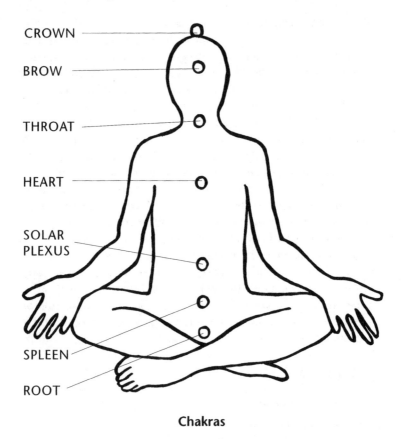

CROWN

BROW

THROAT

HEART

SOLAR
PLEXUS

SPLEEN

ROOT

Chakras

can find ways of using them to explore character as well as performer.

Move up into the spleen chakra – around your kidneys and ovaries.

This is the chakra that affects your feelings of connection with others.

Feel your intimacy with others.

Explore your feelings and emotional needs.

This is the chakra associated with taste.

Then into the solar plexus.

Here, concentrate on your mental energy, will-power, your control over yourself and over others.

This is the chakra associated with sight.

On to the heart.

This is lovingness, trust and harmony, all the things we associate with the heart. This is the chakra associated with touch. It is also your flexibility, your openness to change and it is your balance.

Check your balance again.

Monitor yourself from the ground up.

Now move on.

Upwards to the throat chakra.

This is the chakra that affects your abilities at communication whether they are thoughts or feelings. This is a vital one for the actor as it is the key to your creativity and to your breathing. This is also the chakra associated with hearing.

On next to the head and the brow chakra.

This is your third eye and the chakra that relates to your sixth sense. This is the chakra of fine-tuned awareness. It relates to your overview of yourself, of life and of the world around you.

Finally the crown chakra at the top of your head.

This is the centre of your compassion, altruism and sense of harmony. It affects your ability to see yourself in others. The point of release for all your channelled energy through your body.

Now it is time to explore the chakras in action.

Remember the first workshop we did all that time ago.

Find your feet.

Work all those bones and joints and plant yourself firmly on the floor of the workshop space.

Feel the energy flowing through your body from your feet placed on the ground, up through your chakras and out through your crown.

Remember all the physical work you did in the early workshops in the first part of the programme and relate that to your chakras as you monitor your body.

Begin to move around the room on the grid.

Find your magic neutrality as you move.

Be led by different chakras and by the senses related to them. Combine the energy centre of the chakras with the alertness of the associated sense.

Start with the base chakra and your sexuality and your sense of smell.

Then your spleen – connected with intimacy and taste.

On to your solar plexus with will-power, control and sight.

Next your heart, with lovingness, with touch, but most importantly with balance.

Your throat chakra is next with communication and also hearing, listening as important to communication as speaking.

Now we leave the five senses and move on to the brow chakra with its connectedness to the world around and its association with the sixth sense.

Finally the crown chakra, bringing you into harmony with yourself and with others, the group coming together as an ensemble as you move.

Keep that flow of energy, as you move around the room, feel connected with the ground, the movement of the globe, and at one with your Antipodean performer somewhere on the other side of the world.

Finish by relating this work to character. Choose a character and explore them in terms of their chakras, or alternatively work through the chakras in creating a character. Perhaps Falstaff in *The Merry Wives of Windsor* is led by his base chakra with its sexuality and sense of smell, or Juliet's heart chakra leads as she waits for Romeo and calls on the 'fiery-footed steeds'.

Chapter Eighteen

BOX OF EMOTIONS

This workshop will take a little preparation. You will need a small box. Cut or tear up pieces of paper and on each one write an emotion or a human quality. Fold the pieces of paper and place them in the box. Place the box in the middle of the room. The range of emotions is endless and the differences between them, as we shall see, are subtle and complicated. Here are a few to start you off:

love	anger	happiness
lust	jealousy	delight
pride	irritation	dread
envy	innocence	contentment
hatred	fear	stoicism
grief	terror	covetousness
resignation	guilt	vengefulness

You will think of others and may come up with some that are especially relevant to a project you are working on.

Make a circle around the edge of the space.

Sit down.

In the middle of the space is the box.

Inside the box are pieces of paper, each with a word written on it.

Go to the centre of the room, take out a piece of paper.

Read the word written on it, then screw up the paper and discard it.

Slowly the emotion that has been given to you will consume your entire body.

From deep in the bowels of your being, this emotion will take over your every thought and action.

Eventually you will personify that emotion.

Let it happen slowly.

Work through your body methodically.

Inside and out.

Foot to head.

Head, heart, groin.

Like Lady Macbeth, become filled 'from crown to toe top full of direst cruelty', or whatever other emotion you have drawn from the box.

After each participant has taken their personification as far as you feel it can go, let them relax and ask the rest of the group which emotion they think was being expressed. Identifying the emotions is far from easy, even for the most seemingly obvious of them. As you go, discuss similarities and differences. How can you tell an emotion from the externals of action and appearance? Though working intuitively, we are now bringing thought and the mind to bear on the interpretation of what is being done.

The Elizabethans had a concept of humours. This was a medical theory that there were four distinct liquids or humours in the human body. These were blood, phlegm, yellow bile (choler) and black bile (melancholy). The humours needed to be kept in balance or else a person would become melancholic, choleric, phlegmatic or sanguine. We now think of the idea of humours in relation to the plays of the English writer Ben Jonson, many of whose comic characters are built around the ill balance of their humours. A balance of the humours resulted in a healthy mind and a healthy body. Jonson's characters were far from balanced. This workshop takes the Ben Jonson idea and applies it more widely to every type of emotion.

So far we have worked with the raw emotion without motive, reason or object. Next, we will bring a dynamic into the situation and create emotional couplings. We will start with two obvious and opposite emotions: love and hate.

Find a space in the room.

As you stand there you will be gripped by an all-consuming hatred.

It comes from the pit of your stomach, taking over every molecule of your body and every thought in your head.

Hatred will course through your body like a humour.

It will begin to feel so strong that it moves you around the room.

Let this go on for as long as you can without exhausting your actors. Constantly reinforce the idea. It is usually possible to go on for longer than you might think. When you think the moment is right:

Let the hatred leave your body bit by bit until only the memory of it is left.

Return to neutral.

Relax.

A feeling of all-consuming love is going to grow in your heart.

It will glow in every part of your mind and body.

Love will take you over.

It will move you around the room.

And having moved you around the room it will leave again and allow you to return to yourself.

We have worked with the suggestion of locating the core of these emotions in parts of the body. These you can also relate to chakras and you can find different parts of the body for different emotions. Now we can bring the two emotions we are working with together and create a dynamic in the room.

Half of the group move to one end of the room.

The other half to the other.

The first half are going to be filled with hatred for the other half.

This can, of course, be quite unpleasant. Be prepared for the worst. When the idea has exhausted itself, work the other way round. Then do the same thing with love. This will have been very tiring if done well and so this is a good time to take a break and discuss things so far. How does the experience of love and the experience of hate change when it has an object? How does it feel to be that object? Where does the movement come from? Which is easier to perform? Which is easier to observe? What is truthful and what is false? Where exactly is the emotion first located in the body and what are its effects as it moves from one part to another? Which parts does it reach first?

Return to the box and fill it once more with emotions. These may be the same or different. You may have two boxes, one full of one emotion and the other full of another. You may choose emotions that are suited to a particular exploration. Devotion and disgust might feed off each other with Hamlet and Ophelia; happiness and jealousy might work together, as with John and Winston on Robben Island.

Find a partner.

Each takes a different emotion from the box (or one from each box).

Work together on personifying the emotions.

Your partner's emotion feeds yours – love and hate; desire and terror; anxiety and contentment.

Start slowly.

Finish big.

The closer you get to each other the greater will be the emotional response.

Of course, not all the emotions will be opposites and some may be very similar. The participants may need to spend time thinking and discussing what the word they have actually means. What is fear? How does it differ from terror? What is contentment? Some emotions may lend themselves to movement more than others. Some may demand movement or it may be that the combination of emotions causes movement. We will end this workshop with the physicalised emotions creating the patterns in the room. Choose a piece of music to give a sound pattern to work to, as I said in Chapter Seven, something with a pulse.

Now distil the physicality of your emotion to a few simple, essential movements.

Work on them with your partner.

Once you are confident, go to opposite ends of the space and sit on chairs.

When the music starts, begin to be taken over by the emotion your partner instils in you.

Use that vocabulary of movement.

As the music builds, pattern the room with emotions.

Chapter Nineteen

ONE TO TEN AND BEYOND

Through the course of the previous workshops we have been developing discipline in our actors and cultivating internal self-control. In this and the next workshops, as the conscious mind of the performer is encouraged to intervene in the creation of performance, we will bring internal and external control together.

This is a workshop about precision, about the avoidance of generalisation and the achievement of the specific. It is also about pushing performance to extremes, creating awareness of gradation and variation in performance. The central exercise can be applied to any work you undertake. We will start with the body and with a return to the grid.

WALKING TO SCALE

Find a space in the room.

Begin to walk around the room on the imaginary grid.

Walk as easily and comfortably as you can.

Use as little energy as possible.

Walk at your natural pace.

Think of this as the number one on a scale of one to ten.

This is your normal walking pace.

You are going to begin to slow down.

Think of ten as the slowest it is possible for you to walk.

Begin to get slower.

You are at two.

Slower still to three.

Even slower to four.

Five.

Now you are halfway between your normal pace and the slowest speed possible.

On to six.

Then seven . . . eight . . .

Now nine. This is almost as slow as it is possible for your body to move but not quite.

And to ten.

Your body could not move any slower.

This will not be a steady progression. Actors may be inclined to slow down quickly on the first two or three numbers and leave little in reserve. Over time as this work is repeated, and even over the course of this one workshop, they will begin to develop awareness, control and discipline, monitoring, thinking about and adjusting their work. Play with the speed of command and first run rapidly through the numbers and then much more slowly.

Begin the journey back to one.

Remember you are at ten.

Nine . . . eight . . . seven . . . six . . .

Now five.

You are halfway towards your normal pace, the pace you started with.

Four . . . three . . . two . . .

And one.

You are walking at your starting pace around the grid.

Allow time for this pace to re-establish itself. Check it for truthfulness, neutrality and centring.

Now we will go the other way.

If this is one, we are going towards ten, which is the fastest you can walk.

One . . . two . . . three . . . four . . .

Five. Halfway again, in the other speed direction.

Six . . . seven . . . eight . . . nine . . .

Ten.

You are now walking as fast as you can around the room.

Make sure that it is walking. The activity has not changed, only the speed. Everything else should be the same.

Now you have two scales. One to ten getting faster. One to ten getting slower. In the middle is the neutral one, the normal walking pace of the performer. Work with the area where these two scales meet and one is in the middle, from three on the fast scale, say, through one to five on the slow scale.

Next apply the same principle to the voice. This should be done standing, with the group evenly spaced in the room.

SPEAKING SCALE

Choose a line of text.

This can be from any text you are familiar with.

A whole line.

Speak the line at a conversational level.

As if to the person nearest you.

Breathe easily.

Be relaxed.

Repeat the line.

Monitor the rhythm, diction and tone of what you are doing.

The starting point is important because everything that is done refers back to it.

You are speaking at one on a scale of one to ten.

Ten is the quietest you are able to speak.

Let's move to two.

Three . . . four . . . five . . .

You are halfway to the quietest you can speak.

On to six . . . seven . . . eight . . . to nine. Almost there.

And to ten.

You are saying the line as quietly as you can.

Only the loudness has changed.

Everything else – tone, rhythm, diction – is the same.

Bring your voice back through the numbers to one, the starting point. The vocal level should be exactly where it was when you started and the progression back to it smooth, a perfect increment, build, glissando.

This may be a good moment to stop, relax and discuss before going on to the other way on a scale where one is a normal speaking voice and ten is the loudest it is possible to speak. This should be easy, unforced and spoken, not shouted, maintaining tone, rhythm and diction. As control develops you can work across the scale as we did with the walk.

Speak the line as quietly as possible.

You are at ten.

Gradually increase the volume until you come to your normal vocal level.

From ten to nine . . . eight . . . seven . . . six . . . five . . . four . . . three . . . two . . . one.

You are where your voice is most at ease.

Now to the ten that is your loudest spoken voice.

As the workshop progresses you can try starting at any number, a quiet three for instance or a loud five, and move in any direction. The same can be done with the walk. You might like to combine the walking and the speaking scales. Walk at a slow four and speak at a loud seven. Play with combinations of vocal and physical work, syncopating the voice to the body and the body to the voice. Find ways, in Hamlet's phrase, of suiting the word to the action and the action to the word.

Numbers have the advantages of neutrality and variety. You could work on a shorter scale, say one to five, with less experienced performers; or you could work on a longer scale, say one to twenty or even a hundred, for especially able performers or especially delicate work. Numbers are, for the most part, without emotional significance, though in some cultures individual numbers have associations with good and bad fortune. Numbers are also ever extendable. An actor may feel that they are speaking as quietly or walking as slowly as possible when they reach ten, but you can then move on to eleven, twelve or beyond and demonstrate how much further it is possible to go. Try this using the application of scale to emotion. Choose an emotion to work with, say anger.

SCALE OF EMOTIONS

Find a space in the room.

Be comfortable, relaxed, neutral.

You are going to get angry.

From one to ten you are going to get angrier.

One is the least angry you can be.

Ten is the angriest.

Begin to count out loud. Here we start from zero, because zero is nothing, neutral, while one is something.

Zero . . . one . . . two . . . three . . . four . . . five . . .

You are now halfway to being as angry as you can be.

Six . . . seven . . . eight . . . nine . . . ten.

You are now as angry as you can be.

And you are going to get even angrier.

Eleven . . . twelve . . .

There is always further to go, extremes to be reached. Sometimes it is useful to go even into realms of the grotesque or the caricature so as to find the truth behind it.

Let your performers take control of the scales themselves. Start them off but do not count out aloud. Let them take over. This is a good moment for observation. Divide the group in two and have each show to the other. How clear is the work? How identifiable is the scale? How far can things be pushed to extremes? If you are working on a text or with characters, apply the scales to the material you are working on. Hamlet says he is 'proud, revengeful and ambitious'. To what degree is he each of these on your chosen scale? Joan La Pucelle talks of herself as being 'virtuous and holy'. How virtuous and holy is she and how can you combine these two qualities in a single exercise? Use scale work to help you to explore and to control the complexity of character.

Chapter Twenty

PLAY

For children, play is about learning and socialisation. As childhood comes to an end, so children put play behind them. But for actors play is something to be returned to and an ability to play is something to be relearned.

Many of the workshops in this book have their root in childhood play and children's games. Clive Barker wrote an influential book on theatre games in the 1970s, which brings the worlds of play and playmaking together. As we saw with blind man's buff, many games are common to every childhood culture in every part of the world. Every actor in your workshop, wherever they are from, will have spent many hours playing games as a child. Their early world will have been a playground. As they moved on to school, the playground will have become a circumscribed place and play confined in time and space. As they moved beyond school, the playground would have become a memory and the games of childhood slowly forgotten. The workshop space recreates the playground and a successful workshop should recreate the imaginative, experimental and experiential place within which a child discovers the worlds around them.

I began to work with playground games when I was asked to run a series of workshops at London's Actors Centre on ways to devise physical theatre. One of the workshops had these instructions:

Lie on the floor.

Close your eyes.

Remember your early childhood.

Think of playing games with your friends.

Take yourself back.

Remember.

What games did you play?

How did you play them?

Where?

When?

What was your favourite game?

Remember the rules.

Open your eyes.

Stand up.

Play all the games in the room.

This can be a wild workshop, with inhibitions lost and restraint removed. You may need to keep an eye open for potential injury and like an anxious parent or teacher warn your charges not to get too excited in case someone gets hurt. Everyone should get a chance to instruct the others in a game of their choice. These may be party games, playground games, skipping games, chasing games, circle games, blindfold games, musical games or games of hunting and observation. Some games may be known to everyone in the group while others may be generally known but in different variations. Memory plays tricks with the rules of the games. When you have finished, relax and talk about the games you have played, share memories and recollections. Then choose one of the games and move it into a theatrical context.

From that first workshop at the Actors Centre, one game has become central to all of my work. It is the game that we played in the African village of Fitches Corner – 'grandmother's footsteps'.

Everyone goes to one end of the room except for one person, the grandmother, who goes to the other end and turns her back on the rest of the group.

The object of the game is to touch the grandmother's back without her seeing you move.

The grandmother can turn at any time and if she sees you moving as she turns, you are sent back to the beginning.

Off you go.

I have used this game in many countries and in many continents. For Theatre Nomad it is the beginning exercise of any project. We return to it again and again in any one of an infinite number of variations. We have used it to create entire scenes – the opening of our first production of *Macbeth* – to refresh ourselves, to create instant ensembles, to explore character and gender and to release our imaginations. It is the simplest of games but can lead to the most complex of results. Every country we have travelled to plays it. In England it is called 'grandmother's footsteps' or simply 'statues'. For North Americans it is 'red light green light' and the 'grandmother' is a stop light that shouts 'Red light' as she turns towards the other players and 'Green light' as she turns back. 'What's the time Mr Wolf', *lupo della ore* in Italy, is similar with the 'wolf' shouting times of the day which allow movement in the other players or 'Dinner time' which allows the 'wolf' to move and catch the others.

Played simply at the start of a workshop with a new group of performers, grandmother's footsteps is a perfect way for everyone to learn all the names in the room and for you as a workshop leader to spend some time observing the group you will be working with. Play the basic game a few times and then variations. The variations are endless. Here are a few to get you started.

Try working in pairs or in groups. This can become very competitive and strategies will be worked out within the groupings as the game progresses. You might want to allow time before the game begins for such strategies to be thought up. Leaders may emerge or groupings may find ways of working cooperatively. Some people may work in tight groups clasped together and gliding like one entity across the space. Others may make crocodile chains, or put the biggest at the front to hide the smallest behind.

Play the game in character. For the nomads this worked especially well while preparing for our production of *The Tempest* using Prospero as the grandmother being advanced on by the other characters in the play.

You can play with gender, having your male performers as females and your female performers as males, something we will explore in a later workshop.

Play with age. You can have everyone be 110 years old or perhaps just seven. Or you can have everyone age as they move the length of the room, travelling through time as well as space. The starting point might be ten years old and the finishing point ninety. Make sure that this is disciplined and detailed, using all that has been learned in previous workshops. Every part of the performer should age – the breath, senses and mind as well as the body – as the grandmother is approached and that ageing should be lost and energy restored on being sent back to the start.

Make use of locations and improvise characters. You might be at a teenage birthday party for instance or at a funeral with Death as the grandmother. Finally, have your performers *imagine* that there is somebody there as the grandmother. Here is the chance to find out just how far the imagination of your performers, individually and collectively, have developed. This will show how cooperative your ensemble has become and how competitive some of your performers might be, as they have complete control over their own winning or losing.

A children's game can be endlessly useful in preparing for performance. Grandmother's footsteps is my favourite because the playing of it contains so much. The game uses the body and voice and requires control of balance. Actors explore the space as they play. There are rules and there is infinite variety. The actors work both individually and as an ensemble, going on a journey that is itself a narrative with a beginning, incidents and an ending. The simplicity of the rules of the game allows for a rich complexity of outcome.

You might choose a different game to work with. You might use living statues or musical chairs. You might find a game that has specific uses for a project or play on which you are working. Hopscotch was one such game for me.

Hopscotch is an age-old children's game that is found in every corner of the world. The game was first played not by children but by Roman soldiers on hopscotch 'courts' over a hundred feet long. The soldiers would travel across the squares of the court wearing full armour and carrying their kit on their backs. Soldiers today, and footballers, do something similar, hopping and jumping from car tyre to car tyre.

Presumably children imitated the soldiers' training exercise and created the game that is now played everywhere. Each country has its own variation on the devising of the hopscotch court as the nomads found when we used the game in devising *La Pucelle*, our performance about Joan of Arc. With actors from three different countries, we used the game to access childhood worlds. Only as we researched did we find that the game also provided us with a transition from Joan's being a child to her being a soldier, as the game transformed back into a military exercise. Our actors were from England, France and Hungary and each played hopscotch in a different way. The day after we first played the game, one of our actors, Lisa Payne, saw a group of children playing it on her way to rehearsal and we incorporated what she had seen into our work.

The English version is the simplest. You will need a piece of chalk and a pebble.

HOPSCOTCH

Draw a hopscotch court on the floor.

The first player stands behind the starting line and tries to toss the pebble into square 1.

They then hop over square 1 to square 2 and then continue hopping all the way to square 10.

When the squares are side by side, place two feet down, one in each square.

Turn and hop back again to square 2.

Pause to pick up the pebble.

Hop in square 1 and then hop out of the court.

Pass on the pebble to the next player.

The pebble is thrown from 1 to 10 on each successive turn.

A player is 'out' or misses their turn if the pebble does not land on the right square, if they tread on the chalk lines or if they fail to hop into the right squares.

The first player to complete all the squares is the winner.

There are many variations. Often the court has a destination. English courts have had 'London' written in the finish square since the original Roman soldiers played the game. In Bolivia, where the game is called *la thunkuna*, you travel through time as well as space, with squares and triangles representing the days of the week. France has two distinct versions of the game which our French Joan, Laure Salama, taught us. One, *l'escargot*, has a spiral court, as complex as a labyrinth and requiring strategy as well as

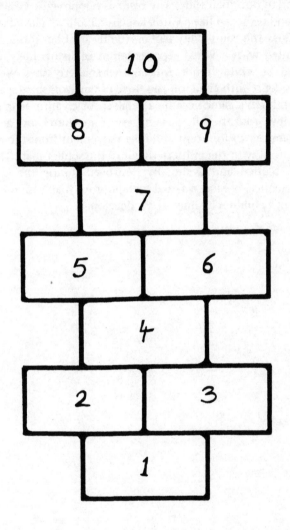

Hopscotch

skill and luck to win. The other, *marelles*, became important to us in working on Joan's life. The court is a journey to heaven or to hell, and is shaped like a Christian church. As we played the game and drew the court every day on the floor of our room, we were presented with a visual representation of Joan's life, her belief system, her childish moments and her soldierly ones. We created Joan's court with chalk on the floor of our workshop space. This one children's game became a catalyst for creating Joan's world. From it we took the religious imagery of the church and developed a vocabulary of innocent childlike movement from the hopping to contrast with the military rigour of the soldier Joan. The chalk court, scuffed and eventually destroyed during the course of performance, became a visual metaphor for Joan's journey. From playing a children's game, a play developed.

Chapter Twenty-one

THE SALT LABYRINTH

At the heart of the labyrinth is the Minotaur. Daedalus built the labyrinth for the Cretan King Midas and it was into its passages that, every nine years, seven young men and seven young women from Athens would be sent as a sacrificial tribute to Midas from his vanquished enemy King Aegeus. Half-man, half-bull, the Minotaur tore to pieces all that entered the labyrinth. No one ever returned. Aegeus' son Theseus resolved to kill the Minotaur, and so end the cycle of death and avenge his father. To aid him in his quest, Ariadne, daughter of King Minos, gave him a sword and a skein of thread. Attaching one end of the thread to the entrance, Theseus entered the labyrinth, unravelling the rest as he journeyed to its centre. Once there, he slew the Minotaur in a fight and then retraced his steps by following the thread to what was now the labyrinth's exit, for the entrance and exit of a labyrinth are one and the same. It is said that on the Greek island of Delos a dance has been performed from ancient to modern times, the Geranos, a dance that recreates Theseus' labyrinthine journey.

Since the original at Minos, labyrinths and mazes (the words are virtually interchangeable) have been found in every culture and in every corner of the globe. The hero of Chris Zithulele Mann's play *Ihuthula – Heart of the Labyrinth* says of a voice in the night:

> Its tongue flickered lightly against my ear,
> And once, twice, three times it prophesied.
> No man, it whispered, will ever be king
> Who has not traced the labyrinth to its core.

These next exercises use the concept of the labyrinth as a way of making the transition between actual space and imagined space. In the previous workshops we have explored ways of using the stage space most effectively, defining that space, creating patterns and relationships within it, and using the movements of

1

2

3

4

5

6

7

8

Salt Labyrinth

9

the actors and their physicality to exploit the possibilities of the stage space to the full. Now we are moving into the realm of the performer's (and by extension the audience's) imagination, where it is possible to create any world and transcend the limitations of the acting space. This is the realm of Shakespeare's 'wooden O', where the actor takes up his injunction to work on 'imaginary forces'. Shakespeare asks: '. . . can this cockpit hold / The vasty fields of France?'

These workshops answer Shakespeare's rhetorical question, taking us beyond the boundaries of the workshop space into a myriad of other worlds.

This Salt Labyrinth derives from performances by the dancer and choreographer Jane Turner and one of the beauties of the workshop is that it is also a complete performance in itself by and for those taking part.

You will need some salt and a container to pour it from, whether it is the original packet or a jug or can. The more salt you have, the bigger your labyrinth can be. You could use sand, and in the open air that might be preferable, but salt pours well, is easily controlled and can be quickly removed without causing mess or damage.

The first task is to draw your labyrinth on the floor with the salt. This can be done by the workshop leader or delegated to one or more of the workshop participants. Slowly, as you take on the role of Daedalus, the labyrinth will come into being before your eyes. Take care to observe the space you are working in, positioning your labyrinth to allow equal room around it in all directions and having its centre at the centre of your room. Those not involved in the making of the labyrinth can sit on the periphery of the space and watch while within that space a new world is created. Here is Jane Turner's labyrinth.

> When you are ready, enter the labyrinth.
>
> Find your way to the centre and return.
>
> It is a simple as that.
>
> You can stop whenever you need to.
>
> There is no rush.

This is a very internalised exercise that should be given as much time as it needs. Thought and contemplation are the key as the performer journeys to the centre of the performance space, and to the centre of their own physical and inner worlds. Some actors will be tentative in their approach; others rush to the centre and back more than once. Each will have a different method of negotiating the labyrinth and each will imagine it in a different way. These differences will create changing dynamics and shifting patterns of movement, overlapping imagined worlds and a variety of inter-actions (or lack of them) between the participants.

Once the energy begins to drop and all the participants have experienced the journey into and out of the labyrinth, bring the group together on the periphery of the labyrinth and lead a discussion on what has been experienced. Some will have found it a difficult and uncomfortable experience, others will have found it joyous and liberating; some will have been aware of everyone else in the room, others will have had a completely private experience. For some the labyrinth may have been no bigger than its physical reality, for others it may have taken on very different scales and shapes and sizes. Some may have been happy at the labyrinth's centre, others will have wanted to escape as soon as possible. All will have entered a world beyond that of the work-shop room and into the realm of the imagination.

I first saw the Salt Labyrinth when Jane used it for an improvised performance that she had made in London and Halifax, Nova Scotia. Since then she and I have used it in many situations, most memorably at the National Centre for the Arts in Banff, Canada, where it was the first workshop in a process of adapting John Buchan's novel *Sick Heart River* for the stage. The novel is about two men's different journeys to the far north of Canada and simultaneously to the depths of their souls. It is about their eventual meeting and their separate returns. The labyrinth seemed a perfect metaphor for this narrative and a way of transferring it to the stage. Journeys are at the heart of every play and the labyrinth can be used as a metaphor for these journeys. The entrance to the labyrinth can be the entrance to the world of the play, the first step of the journey – both narrative and emotional – that each character takes or the beginning of the story in which all are involved.

Having done the exercise once, it can now be repeated in a number of different ways, to develop skills, to build relationships within the group, to explore themes and to explore text. Here are some suggestions.

Performers can work singly, in pairs or in groups, helping or hindering each other. They can be allowed to interact with each other.

You can use the labyrinth to help your performers develop their orientation, memory and sense of direction by having to retrace their *exact* steps without recourse to Ariadne's skein of thread. This is an excellent way of creating a precise use of patterning on stage and of spatial memory.

The work can be kept private or your performers can be questioned about their experiences by you or by each other. What is it like in the centre of the labyrinth? What was the journey to the centre like? What is it like to be alone?

The centre of the labyrinth can represent a physical goal or destination – Prospero's journey to the island, say, or Caliban's to the depths of his cave; Oedipus' return to Thebes or Faustus' descent into hell. The centre can be an emotional or psychological destination – Ophelia's decline into madness or Viola's transformation into Cesario.

The journey can be to the inner self of the performer (something almost inevitable when the performer enters the labyrinth for the first time) or it can be a journey to the inner self of a character. Perhaps it is at the centre of the labyrinth that Claudius says his prayer and it is there that Hamlet overhears him. Perhaps it is where Macbeth decides to kill Banquo.

The labyrinth can be used to represent narrative; objects or written tasks can be placed in the centre of the labyrinth as a catalyst for thought or action; lines of dialogue or odd words of text can be added to the exercise. One possibility is to have words or phrases scribbled on notes left in the centre of the labyrinth; another is to have them written with a finger in the salt.

There are, as so often, endless possibilities. They are limited only by your imagination.

Finish the workshop by sweeping away the salt. This should be a collective act and done with care and precision. The actors' space is a sanctified one and should always be prepared with care and treated with respect, something any performer from an Eastern tradition will know. In Eastern theatres, the cleaning and organisation of the space is as important as the performances that happen on or within it. Shoes are left outside or to one side of the performance space. There are great virtues in following such practices in the use of your workshop space. Ensure the space is clean, neat, tidy and organised before you begin. Use your participants in this preparation and make them attentive to the care, order and cleanliness of their space. The reasons are many, from the practicality of ensuring there is nothing dirty, irritating or dangerous on the floor, to the removal of distractions and the creation of a mutual respect for a shared working, living and playing environment. The stage is a private space within a public one. In many cultures it is treated with the respect of a private home or a religious sanctuary. The removal of shoes before entering the space is common in many theatrical traditions. With the nomads we have our own tradition of blessing our space with water wherever we perform, cleansing the stage of past performances and allowing a moment of focus and private thought to all the performers before the performance commences.

As the salt is swept to one side, the imagined worlds it helped create will remain as memories in the minds and imaginations of all the participants. On the now bare stage begin the exercise once more, this time without the physical image of the salt to guide the actors.

When you are ready, enter the labyrinth.

Find your way to the centre and return.

It is a simple as that.

You can stop whenever you need to.

There is no rush.

Jane's maze, like that on the floor of Chartres Cathedral, is a classic single-path maze. There are also puzzle mazes in which one can become lost for hours, days, indeed for ever. Such mazes can take many forms. Some, like one in which I became lost in Prague while making the golem performance, are made of mirrors. The labyrinth crosses the boundaries of real and imagined space. Drawn in salt it is a physical reality within the boundaries of the workshop room. But on entering it, the performer embarks on a journey into the imagination, allowing the labyrinth to take on any quality or dimension.

Having emptied the space of an actual maze, we can now let imaginations loose to create entirely illusory ones with no physical boundaries.

Stand at the side of the space.

You are on the outside of a puzzle maze.

You have to find your way to the centre of the maze.

This centre can be indicated by something – a pebble, a box with something inside of it, a flower or a shell, say. The object can be something suggestive of a text or idea on which you are working.

Having found your way to the middle of the maze, you must then find your way out again. This is perhaps more difficult than finding your way to the centre in the first place, as you have to recall the maze they have invented and retrace your steps in reverse.

The exercise can be done one at a time or with everyone working simultaneously. If the latter, performers should work ignoring their fellows, staying in their own imagined worlds. This way, the space is filled with as many different mazes as there are performers. Without prompting, mazes will be created in two, three, even four dimensions; out of foliage, glass, ice, or bricks; noisy mazes; pitch black mazes; mazes of terror and mazes of joy. All will demonstrate what Peter Ackroyd in his novel *The Plato Papers* calls 'the sanctity of mazes and mirrors'. There are people who suffer from a pathological fear of mazes. The condition is called labyrinthitis. I have yet to come across it in a performer, but as with so much else that can be unexpected in a workshop, be prepared to encounter it.

> Describe your maze to the rest of the group.
>
> If you have observed other mazes, what did you see?

For the final part of this maze workshop, work in pairs to create collectively imagined spaces.

> Find a partner.
>
> Spend time devising a joint maze.
>
> Stand at either side of the space.
>
> Each of you has to enter the maze from opposite ends, find each other and come out together.

Finish by bringing all these imaginary mazes together. This is good done to music. Have pairs, either one at a time or in overlapping relay, recreate their mazes and search for each other. Like the inhabitants of the island of Delos with their Geranos, you are recreating Theseus' journey in the labyrinth or, with the music playing, echoing the story of Orpheus and Eurydice.

Chapter Twenty-two

DREAMTIME

There was a dreamtime, the Aboriginal peoples of Australia believe, when the ancestors created the landscape as they walked the world. The world was literally walked into existence. With this workshop you can walk whole worlds into existence, from Illyria to Prospero's island, from Elsinore to the Cherry Orchard, from Robben Island to Thebes, from the battlefields of Joan of Arc to the concentration camps of Nazi Germany.

We start, as so often, with the grid. This is a way of disciplining movement in the room but it also works in at least two other ways. Firstly, the infinite number of grid squares that it can create makes for an infinity of *imagined* space within the finite *stage* space.

Performances happen not only within the three dimensions of space but also within the fourth dimension of time. Like the poet William Blake, actors can see whole worlds in the grain of sand that is the stage, and also hold eternity in an hour's traffic of stage time.

Secondly, there is something hypnotic about the patterning created by walking on the grid. The walking on the grid becomes something like a process of self-hypnosis. This is one reason why it is important to start slowly and rhythmically.

Hypnosis is very like acting: indeed, some researchers into the psychology of hypnosis believe that hypnosis *is* acting and that acting *is* hypnosis. Both result in changes in sensations, perceptions, thoughts and behaviour. In hypnotism, as in these workshops, such changes are brought about by relaxation accompanied by suggestion. Suggestions are continually reinforced through repetition to maintain the trance-like state. A hypnotised person, like an actor, is fully conscious throughout everything that they are doing, but they are in an altered state of consciousness. Usually hypnotism is 'induced' through a process of relaxation, but a 'suggestible' person, or a person who has often been hypnotised, can respond to hypnotic suggestion without hypnotic induction.

At Middlesex University in England I ran workshops with the psychologist David Marks to explore the relationship between hypnosis and acting. The light hypnotic trance induced in the actors led them to do some things that were of no surprise to anyone who has taken part in a drama workshop but which non-actors would have found difficult or foolish, such as thinking of themselves as a colony of apes. Other activities went far beyond what might be expected in a performance workshop. Two actors with a real fear of heights stood on the shoulders of fellow actors and were walked across the room to greet each other. One of them was Becky Hall. This is how she described the experience: 'I have vertigo and yet I'm standing on Richard's shoulders. And the magic is, I'm smiling with my arms open and looking at another woman who I know also has vertigo who is standing on another's actor's shoulders and we are reaching out to each other in a cosmic embrace.'

Acting can be thought of as a form of self-hypnosis, with the workshops as an induction process that only needs to be touched on in a warm-up or moment of focus before a performance to come into play.

As we begin this workshop we will set up the slow, rhythmic repetition of walking around the grid. Gradually, we will bring in suggestions or instructions that will create the altered state of consciousness that acting requires. The tone of voice in these workshops is important. Walk among the participants as you speak. Keep your voice as quiet as is possible to still effectively get across what you are saying. Speak simply so that a few words hang in the air.

Walk around the grid.

Halve that speed.

Actors will always move too quickly. Remember that we are working in both space and time. We are creating our own space and time as we work. This is why breaking the speed, rhythm and spatial awareness of the workroom itself is crucial so as to liberate your performers into whatever imagined space and time they might become a part of creating.

DESERT

Feel your body in the space.

Be aware of your movements; your feet on the ground; the articulation of your joints.

Be aware of your senses; the feel of the floor, of the air; the smell of the room; the sights and sounds around you, the tastes in your mouth.

Inhabit the room as you walk.

As you travel, the room is going to disappear and you will find yourself walking in the desert.

It is a hot desert and as you walk the air is going to get even hotter.

Feel the sand underneath your feet.

It is falling away as you walk.

It is hot.

Feel the sun and the hotness of the air.

How is it changing as you walk? How is it affecting your joints and your movements?

Run through your senses.

Breathe in the hot air, feel it affect your vision, your hearing, your taste.

As you walk you become more and more exhausted.

You are getting more tired; the sun is getting hotter.

I first devised this workshop when we were adapting Charlotte Delbo's writings about surviving the concentration camps for Theatre Nomad's performance *Survivors*. For that original workshop we created the desolate world of the camps. For this version of the workshop we are using a simple image of a desert, an environment which every actor will comprehend even if few may have experienced it. The suggestion of the detail is important, as are the constant reminders of the different ways in which an environment may affect the body. The reminders of different and perhaps more neglected senses are important too. Suggestion is more important than instruction. In all of these visualisation exercises it is important to release the performers' imagination and not impose on it. Everything should be left to the individual imaginations within the room. During the workshop we will slowly bring these imaginations together to form a collectively imagined world, just as we created paired worlds in the maze workshop. We think of visualisation, but that implies just one sense, sight, creating a world. This exercise is multi-sensory; it is *aisthetic*, using all the senses to perceive an imagined world. As the performers create the world internally it will appear externally to anyone observing them. You might like to divide the group during the workshop to allow for this observation. Meanwhile, back in the desert:

> So tired are you all, that one in the group may collapse with exhaustion. If they do, the rest of the group has to get them up and moving again.

Here we are both creating a jointly imagined world and building a group dynamic. We are working with what Jerzy Grotowski called 'poor theatre'. Grotowski worked at his Laboratory Theatre in Opole, Poland, from the late 1950s, stripping away everything that he associated with what he called 'rich theatre' until all that were left were the actors. Eventually, he even excluded the audience from his theatre, working, as we are today, with the actors in a closed space.

Keep this exercise going as long as you dare, constantly reinforcing your suggestions as you go. Remind the participants that they are getting ever weaker.

> Just when you think you can go no further, clouds begin to appear in the sky; rain begins to fall; the heavens open and you are drenched with warm, sweet rain.

A short suggestion but one that you should allow time to be enjoyed.

> Relax.
>
> You are back in the workshop room.

This exercise is about releasing the performer's imagination and developing a detailed physical imagination, so that the body really does inhabit the other space, the other world. Suggestion and not instruction is the key. Do not supply any detail; allow the performer's imagination to do that. Performers from different cultures, countries, places will respond differently to the word 'desert', or to the word 'forest' which we use in the next workshop. Let everything come from the mind and body of the performer. Do not impose from the outside. You must guide, suggest and reinforce. When you stop to discuss the exercise among the group is for you to determine, depending on the need to maintain or to break concentration, to diffuse an intense situation or to build creatively upon it. As ensemble-building exercises, these are also ways of finding out about the cultures, backgrounds and experiences of members of the group – some will know deserts maybe, some will know forests, some may have lived above the snowline and some may never have seen snow. This exercise develops the imagination of the performer as an individual and the collective imagination of a group of performers as an ensemble. It can also be used for the imagined creation of specific environments of a play, from the 'vasty fields of France' in Shakespeare's *Henry V* to the confines of Bluebeard's Castle.

Repeat the journey but this time into a world of cold.

COLD

Feel the cold underfoot, in your bones, in your nose and mouth and ears.

Your skin is cold.

The cold is working its way into your bones.

Every breath you take brings cold air into your body.

Your senses are beginning to be affected.

Your sense of touch is changing.

Your sense of sight.

How is your hearing?

Try to keep warm as you travel.

You cannot get any colder and still survive.

Then, when you think you can go no further, the sun comes out.

The imagination is a powerful tool. The actor does not need to have actual experience to be able to imagine a world any more than any other creative artist does. The first piece of music that the composer Joseph Haydn was commissioned to write as a seventeen-year-old was to illustrate a storm at sea. The young landlocked Austrian had never seen the sea, let alone experienced a storm at sea, yet his music was utterly convincing. It was to be more than another forty years before the man who had by then composed so many different worlds with his music journeyed to England. He reached the port of Calais now aged nearly sixty, and saw the sea for the first time. Haydn's crossing of the channel was delayed as a storm raged through the night.

As you work on a text or on devising your performance, the world you are collectively creating will continually develop. This development will continue during a run of performances, actors having little epiphanies while they are performing as they realise and recognise things about their character and the world they inhabit that they had never noticed before. So, while this workshop can be a starting point for creating a dramatic world in the imaginations of the actors, it is also one to return to at regular intervals to monitor the developing richness of that world and to reinforce the discoveries of the imagination.

We have moved from working individually to working collectively as a group during this exercise. This can be useful both for creating a shared world inhabited by all the actors in a production, and also as a way of helping to build and strengthen an ensemble. As a group exercise it can be taken further. On one of our Banff adventures, we created, within the comfortable confines of perhaps the most luxurious dance studio in the world, an imagined journey through the remotest parts of northern Canada. Through the freeing of their collective imaginations, the actors went through extremes of deprivation, cold and trauma. To assist them create the journey in their heads, to 'work their minds' as Shakespeare says in Sonnet 27, numbered notes were places around the studio. As if on a board game, the actors, working as a group for survival, had to find their way from one number to the next. On each note was an instruction – 'you have to cross a crevasse', 'one of you is about to die of cold', 'you find a shelter with food', and so on. These were instructions suggested by the material we were working on. Other material will suggest different instructions in different worlds.

It is also possible to work with the group not as a whole but as a collection of individuals. This we did as the starting point for the nomads' production of *The Tempest*. All the characters in the play inhabit one island but they all think of it differently. Perhaps none of them knows it all. So we created the island in the minds of the actors and then each actor, using odd props and furniture that happened to be in the rehearsal space, recreated their version of the island. We eventually had six or seven imagined versions of the same island superimposed on each other in the same workshop space. Each actor took the rest of the cast on a tour of *their* island. Caliban took us to his cave and the tree in which his mother had been imprisoned; Miranda took us to secret places her father did not know about; Prospero concentrated on his cell and his books, and so on.

Imagined space is Prospero's island, the Athenian forest, Hamlet's ramparts, Winnie's beach, the Cherry Orchard, John and Winston's Robben Island with its own imagined worlds within it. It is the space that exists in the mind of the actor and, by the power of that acting imagination, in the minds, collective and individual, of the audience.

In the dreamtime and dream space of a workshop any world can be walked into existence.

Chapter Twenty-three

TRANSFORMATIONS

What is acting? Edith Evans was once asked how she had managed to play so many different parts. 'I don't really know,' she replied, 'except that I seem to have an awful lot of people inside me.' Sarah Bernhardt believed that it was 'the actor's duty to forget himself of his proper attributes in order to attain those of the part'. The great European acting controversy of the nineteenth century was between the French actor Coquelin who believed that an actor should not feel anything at all and the English actor Henry Irving who believed that an actor should be feeling the very things he is talking about. There are as many theories of acting as there are actors and acting teachers and most of these theories are little more than hunches. Actors, when working at their best, give little thought to what it is they are doing. Psychological investigation into the acting process has been minimal. The neurologist Oliver Sacks was fascinated to watch Robert De Niro on the set of the film of Sacks's book *Awakenings*. He could not fathom what De Niro, the actor, was doing to become Leonard Lowe, a character based upon a real person whom Sacks had known. 'Can a neurological syndrome be acted?' Sacks asked himself. 'Can an actor with, presumably, a normally functioning nervous system and physiology "become" someone with a profoundly abnormal nervous system and behaviour? Can he have the experience – psychological, or indeed, physiological – which would enable him to do this? There can, obviously, be a sort of imitation or mimesis – but this is not acting, this is not the level at which Bob works. He himself had said right at the beginning, "It's never just a method, just a technique – it's a *feeling*. You have to feel what's right, feel it out of your own experience and self-knowledge."' Sacks observed that De Niro, 'let what he knew of the character he was playing sink down into his unconscious and there ferment, unite with his own experiences, powers, imagination, feelings – and only then would they return, become visible, so deeply infused with his own character and subjectivity as to be now an integral part, an expression of, himself . . . I knew how deeply he might identify with the characters he portrayed, but had to wonder now how *neurologically* deep he might go – whether he might actually, in his acting, *become* Parkinsonian, or at least (in an astoundingly controlled fashion) somehow duplicate the neurological state of the patient. Does acting like this, I wondered, actually alter the nervous system?'

The English actor Ralph Richardson said that for him acting was 'to some extent a controlled dream'. The idea of dreaming and controlling those dreams is close to much of the work in this part of the programme. Bottom had a dream, or at least he thought he did, and it was a dream, 'past the wit of man to say what dream it was'. Bottom describes his dream as a vision and this workshop continues our work on visualisation. Bottom's friends run off in fear when they see him with his ass's head, fearing themselves to be haunted. 'Bless thee, Bottom, bless thee! Thou art translated!' says Peter Quince. This workshop comes out of Bottom's translation.

INTO THE FOREST

Take off your shoes.

Make a circle of them in the middle of the room.

Find a space and begin a journey.

Work on the grid around the room.

Halve that speed.

As we have noticed in the previous workshop, it is almost always the case that your performers will walk too fast. A slower speed will allow for a more neutral, comfortable way of walking and so create a better starting point for the transformations to come. Like the induction required to enter a hypnotic trance, the start of this exercise should bring about calmness and relaxation.

As you walk you find yourself in a forest.

The workshop room disappears and you begin to travel further and further, deeper and deeper into the forest.

Feel the vegetation around you and underfoot.

See the sights, hear the sounds, smell the smells, taste the tastes of the forest.

As you travel you get ever deeper and you realise that night is falling and you have to find somewhere to sleep.

Find that safe place for the night.

Make yourself comfortable and fall asleep.

Wake, relax and talk about your forest.

This is a good moment to stop the performers, and go around the group to find out where they have reached on their journey. You will find as many forests as you have performers.

Where was your forest? What was it like? Where did you go to sleep?

These discussion points, as in other exercises, are optional. You might want to keep the concentration by reinforcing the suggestions you make, or break the concentration, which will mean a degree of re-induction when you resume. You may be surprised at how many forests there can be in the same room at the same time. It is important that you prompt as little as possible. The word 'forest' is the key one. Some individuals and some groups may require more help to get their visualisation going. Keep reinforcing with your suggestions and with reminders about the senses and different things that might or could be felt. It is important that your suggestions are used to release the imagination of your performers and not to impose your own vision. You could, with this exercise, create a very specific forest giving every detail to your participants, but it would be your forest and not theirs. This workshop originated in the explorations for Theatre Nomad's production of *A Midsummer Night's Dream*. We wanted to discover a forest for the production that was a world shared by all of us who were working on the play. We had no trees or foliage for our settings. All that the actors had to play with, and the audience to see, was an inflated paddling pool filled with water. Yet all of the actors in their collective imagination, and by extension the audience too in the connection of their imaginations with those of the actors, had to create, at every performance, a very real forest.

We also wanted to explore the forest's magical attributes at transformation. Everyone in the forest is transformed in some way, whether emotionally or physically or both. The workshop now goes on to explore transformation, using the created forests as the suggestive power for that transformation.

THE POOL

Go back to sleep.

In a while you will wake up.

Close by you is a pool of clear, clean water – the circle of shoes.

When you wake, go down to the pool and do the things you do first thing in the morning.

Ignore everyone else.

You are alone in the forest.

While at the pool you catch sight of yourself in the water and realise that you have been transformed in some way overnight.

What is the transformation?

How do you react to it?

Stop.

Sit out.

Relax and recover.

Tell us about your experience.

This can be powerful stuff. We have not said whether the transformation is good or bad. You might want to. Performers are often surprised at what they come up with. The results can be frightening to experience and disturbing to watch or they can just as readily be delightful, life-enhancing and beautiful. We have entered dream worlds but with little if any control over the dreams or nightmares that the suggestive power of the workshop can unleash. It is amazing how spontaneously this can work. It is beyond conscious thought and requires the performer to use their body in a very different way from the previous exercises.

There can be room for observation built into this exercise but that can break the spontaneity and can make the exercise less focused and less intimate and personal. You must decide.

The playwright Noël Greig visited me in South Africa while he was writing his play *At Break of Day*. One of my students asked him what he saw in his head while he was writing. Surprisingly, Noël had never been asked this before. His answer was equally surprising. He said that he sees films in his head, the scenes he is writing fully realised, complete visualisations. Yet Noël is a creature of the theatre and his plays, including the one he was then writing for the nomads, are highly theatrical. Noël sees no contradiction in this. The imagination of the writer is limitless, as is the imaginative power of performer and audience. In the introduction to his best-known play, *Plague of Innocence*, he writes that 'on the most basic level [the play] could be staged with one actor on a bare platform, assuming all the parts and all the narrative. To my mind, this is the most exciting style of performance, since it takes us to the very heart of the actor's skill: the act of transformation, without any of the usual props and disguises. It is the very essence of theatre, the invitation to inhabit two realities simultaneously.'

Chapter Twenty-four

THROUGH THE LOOKING GLASS

This workshop starts with what might appear to be one of the simplest exercises possible: having one performer mirror the actions of another. It is an exercise that can be done with the least experienced of performers, even schoolchildren, but it is also an exercise that can constantly bring results with the most experienced. Mirror work is one of the simplest activities for a pair of performers to do, but it can also be the subtlest and the most sophisticated. The work aids observation, of oneself and of one's partner, and encourages infinite refinement and delicacy of movement and action. Mirror work does not have to be limited to pairs – you can work in any number from trios to large groups – but the pair is the basic and most productive unit and it is the one with which we will start.

HUMAN MIRRORS

Find a partner.

Find your space.

One lead, the other follow.

Make an action.

Follow that action.

Start with something slow and simple.

Make it slower and more simple.

Work fluidly but do not move from the place you are standing on.

Observe carefully.

A moving hand may mean a change of balance, a shift of posture.

Find a repetitive movement to allow more focused observation.

Swap over.

Slowness is of the essence in beginning this work. It is important to remember everything that has been learned in the body workshops in the first half of the programme. The slightest movement of a finger will have repercussions elsewhere in the body. It will be echoed through the arm, monitored by a glance and a momentary turn of the head. There is movement even in stillness. The German choreographer Pina Bausch asks of her dancers that they internalise their dance to the point of stillness so that the body dances inside of itself.

This work then is about both control and observation, but it is also about the unity of mind and body. More than that, this workshop is about the unity of two minds and two bodies working in harmony.

MOVING MIRRORS

Return to stillness.

Become centred and body-neutral.

As before, start slowly and with care.

Now you can begin to move in space, towards or away from your mirror image.

You have two choices: either true mirroring in which the partners will move together or apart; or reverse mirroring when they move in the same direction, that is as your partner takes a step towards you, you take a step back away from them. We will start with the first.

As the distance between you increases make the gestures and movements bigger.

As you become more confident make them smaller.

Swap over again.

Eventually you should reach a point where you can swap between each other with only the slightest indication.

Come back together.

Be neutral.

Now with reverse mirroring.

As your partner steps towards you, take a step back.

And again.

Now in reverse.

Play with this and use it as a variation among all the other moves you have made.

Be ready; anticipate whether you are going to move towards or away from your partner.

Be alert, be very alert.

Take time out to allow pairs to be observed by the rest of the group. If a pair is working well, it should be impossible for the outside observer to detect which of the pair is leading and which is following.

Gradually the performers should expand into the space so that they can work right across it and be able to turn their backs on each other. Once this stage is reached it is possible, like Alice, to step through the looking glass and to 'pretend the glass has gone all soft like gauze, so that we can get through'.

'Why,' said Alice, 'it's turning into a sort of mist now, I declare! It'll be easy enough to get through.'

PLANES OF MOTION

Find a partner.

Find your space.

One moves, the other follows.

This time keep an equal distance between you.

If the lead partner steps forward, the other steps back.

Keep the space between you exact – whether it is half a metre or six metres.

Experiment with different distances.

Begin to move in three dimensions, up and down, back to front, side to side – in every plane of movement.

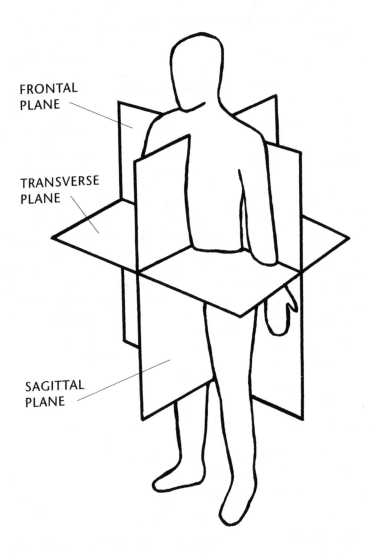

FRONTAL
PLANE

TRANSVERSE
PLANE

SAGITTAL
PLANE

Planes of motion

It can be useful to think of this exercise in anatomical terms. The body can be divided into 'planes of motion'. There are three cardinal planes. A cardinal plane divides the body equally in two through the centre of gravity. So imagine slicing the body in equal halves. The sagittal plane divides the body into left and right as it passes front to back. The frontal plane divides the body into front and back as it passes side to side. The transverse plane divides the body into top and bottom as it passes front to back through the sagittal plane. All these planes pass through the body's centre of gravity. The centre of gravity is an imaginary point where the total weight of the body can be thought to be concentrated. Weight is balanced around the centre of gravity. In a sphere the centre of gravity will be in the very middle, equidistant from any point on the surface. That is why, because of its perfect balance, the slightest touch will set a sphere into motion. A sphere is a symmetrical object. The human body is an asymmetrical object. As we have found in previous workshops, the centring of the body leads to balance and balance leads to ease of movement through the planes of movement.

CENTRES OF GRAVITY

With your partner find each other's centres of gravity.

With your partner work out how the imaginary planes of motion bisect your bodies.

Any movement of the body requires an axis to move around. So for each cardinal plane there is a cardinal axis passing through the body's centre of gravity. The sagittal axis passes through the body front to back. The frontal axis passes through the body side to side. The longitudinal axis passes through the body top to bottom. Your body moves within the planes on the axes of movement.

Explore your centres of gravity and the ways in which you move around them.

Find the planes of movement.

Find the axes of movement.

Explore balanced movement around your centre of gravity.

Which axes are you moving around?

Which planes are you moving along?

Return to the mirror now.

Take a step towards and past each other.

Experiment.

Perhaps touching hands as you revolve into each other's mirror world.

Perhaps moving away from each other, back to back with the occasional glance over your shoulder.

Now it is time to play with all that has been done. Put on a piece of music.

Work to the music.

You will see many things. Allow and encourage the performers to work throughout the space, in close proximity to each other and at a great distance, exploring what is possible and how much detail can be conveyed to each other and followed over the width of the space. Just as with our voice work, it should be possible to convey the tiniest detail across the whole workshop space. Take time out for people to watch each other and find how what is communicated between performers can be communicated to the audience.

You might finish by applying the work to character, giving actors a chance to observe their characterisations as they are mirrored by others, finding centres of gravity for the characters that are inhabiting their bodies, working their characters in every plane of movement and in every part of the space.

Chapter Twenty-five

TANGO

It was a bitterly cold Christmas Eve. On the London railway terminus of St Marylebone, people were hurrying home laden with shopping, presents and expectation. People stared at the destination boards and waited for the announcement of their trains. From the tannoy system the words of the station master were suddenly replaced by a familiar tune. The strains of Johann Strauss's 'Blue Danube Waltz' wafted across the station concourse. From the crowd, figures appeared, similar to yet strangely different from the hundreds of travellers around them. Each had a suitcase in their hand. As the music swelled, these unusual travellers found their lips responding to the sounds in the air. Their destinations began to be dictated by the movements of their lips, pulling them strongly around the station. The travellers began to waltz with each other, joined not by their arms but by a magnetic quality in their lips. The crowds around them withdrew to watch the dance that began to form in front of them. No sooner had the music finished than the travellers were absorbed back into the crowd that filled the void once more. A few minutes of magic had distracted the commuters as they went off for their Christmas celebrations around the country.

It was from the following exercise that this performance was devised.

BODY PARTS

Find a space in the room.

Relax your body and bring yourself to neutral.

Walk on the imaginary grid.

Walk comfortably and easily.

As you walk you are gradually going to be led by different parts of your body.

Your right shoulder is taking control.

Gradually it is going to dictate your movement around the grid.

Gently at first but with increasing strength.

Now that control is going to weaken and you will come back to neutral walking.

Now your left buttock is beginning to take control.

Now your groin.

Now your heart.

Now your right nipple.

Return to neutral.

Continue walking on the grid.

As always, allow time for these changes to develop slowly. To begin with nothing should be sudden.

Slowly your lips are going to lead.

This might start with a little puckering which gradually leads to something much stronger and out of the contol of the performer.

You find your lips are attracted to other lips in the room.

But like magnets, they can only get within, say, six inches of each other before repelling and pushing you apart.

Like first-date rules of an American college you can only get within a few inches of your intended partner.

You are never allowed to touch.

Begin to enjoy this.

Play with it.

Control each other.

Move each other around the room.

One or two of you have especially attractive lips.

Slowly the power fades.

Return to neutral walking.

I once did a fascinating version with armpits when I was exploring atavistic animal-like attraction in humans. The exercise frees up the body. No one walks in neutral, though the achievement of a magically neutral starting point is, as we have seen over these workshops, crucial to the creation of the non-neutrality that is the essence of performance. As well as the waltz performance in Marylebone station, I have used this exercise in the creation of of a tango piece where the lips were so powerful they even brought members of the audience into the performance space. These were emotionally driven but abstract pieces.

The application to the exploring of character is obvious and can be a wonderful way of helping create the physicality of characters from essences of emotional or physical centres. Marlowe's Helen of Troy – the face that launched a thousand ships or Antony's heart that 'hath burst the buckles on his breast', the hands of Romeo and Juliet in 'holy palmer's kiss', the fire in Hero's eye in *Much Ado*, or Lysander and Hermia's hearts 'knitting into one'.

This work brings together emotion with the use of the actor's body in the workshop space. All performance is about the making of patterns in space. As Robert Davidson, the choreographer and master of the low-flying trapeze, puts it, 'The performer leaves traces as they move in the space.' The steps of social dance forms, waltz and tango in the above examples, can give us other matrices and other ways of defining and using the performer's space. The tango is a wonderfully potent tool, bringing together emotion, discipline, use of every part of the body, mirroring and close pair work.

TANGO

Find a partner.

Find your space.

Learn to tango.

The tango was first danced in the brothels of Buenos Aires. It was danced competitively between men, dangerous, threatening, with lives at stake. It was danced to the beat of an African drum: tang-go, tan-go, tan-go. Sometimes it was danced with knives. Then the men began to partner the women and the dance as we know it today was created. The basics of the steps are simple and, like the mirror work we did earlier, one performer leads and the other follows. As with the very first workshop in this programme, we are going to start with the foot.

> Everyone come together and make a circle.
>
> Walk clockwise around the room.
>
> Walk to a beat: tan-go, tan-go, tan-go.
>
> Keep the circle the same size as you walk.

This is not easy. The tendency is for the circle to become smaller very quickly. As with the exercises in Workshop Five, spend time on the precision of this circle. Do not move on until this basic discipline has been achieved.

> Turn and walk the other way.
>
> Notice how you walk.
>
> How your foot is placed on the ground.
>
> How one foot is placed in front of the other.
>
> Change the way you walk.
>
> Place your toes on the ground before your heel.

This too is difficult to do. We are teaching the performers to discipline their bodies and use them in ways very different from the ones they are used to.

> Turn and walk the other way.
>
> Always keep the shape and size of the circle.
>
> With the same step, walk backwards.

This is the first walk of our tango and is the walk of the leader, traditionally the male role.

> Still placing your toes on the floor first, place one foot directly in front of the other as you walk.
>
> Always keep the shape and size of the circle.

This is the second walk of our tango and is the walk of the follower, traditionally the female role.

> With the same step, walk backwards.
>
> With the same step, walk forwards.
>
> Stop.
>
> Find a partner.
>
> Stand in front of each other.
>
> One do the leader step, the other follow.
>
> You are reverse mirroring.
>
> Take yourselves around the room.

Already everyone is tangoing. Next we have to put in a form of the basic tango step modified for our use.

A

> Find a space with your partner in the room.
>
> The leader is going to move backwards.
>
> Moving the right foot first.
>
> One, two, three steps back, on the fourth move the left foot back and to the side (in an L shape).
>
> Bring the right foot to the left to close.

> The follower is going to move forwards in mirror of this.
>
> Moving the left foot first.
>
> One, two, three steps forward, on the fourth move the right foot forward and to the side (in an L shape).
>
> Bring the left foot to the right to close.

B

> The leader is now going to move forwards.
>
> Again moving the right foot first.
>
> One, two steps forward.

Bring the right foot to the left to close.

The follower is going to move backwards in mirror of this.

Again moving the left foot first.

One, two steps backwards.

Left foot to the right foot to close.

We have moved backwards, sideways and forwards if we are leading. We have moved forwards, sideways and backwards if we are following.

Now we are going to do the opposite of the opening L shape to end this basic move.

C

The leader is going to continue to move forwards.

Again right foot first.

One, two steps forwards, the third wth the right foot forwards and to the right side (in an L shape).

Bring the left foot to the right to close.

The follower is going to continue to move backwards.

Again left foot first.

One, two steps backwards, the third with the left foot backwards and to the left side (in an L shape).

Bring the right foot to the left to close.

You should be facing each other in the same mirrored opening position as you started but forward in the space.

Now it is time to join leader and follower together.

The leader's left hand should hold the follower's right shoulder.

The leader's right hand should be in the small of the follower's back, and the follower's left hand on the leader's shoulder.

Move around the room using the tango steps.

This is as much tango as you need to know for now. Do not worry if you find some of it difficult. Learn as much of the language of the dance as you can. Above all, play with it. You can add and subtract as many steps as you like. Pause in suspension whenever you like. Play with moving in and out of the mirror.

There are endless pieces of music to choose from, and the works of the Argentinian Astor Piazzolla are a good place to start. Piazzolla invented *Tango Nuevo* – New Tango – and his pieces have the innate theatricality of dance music. They are often scored for small groups of instruments, which make them ideal for this sort of work.

One more exercise:

All the leaders should go to one side of the room.

All the followers to the other.

When the music starts, each of the leaders can go and choose a follower and move with them around the room.

The tango is an improvisatory dance. Even with the very basic steps we have learned in this workshop, it is possible to improvise in an infinite variety of ways. Improvise with the basic steps of the tango and bring in as many of the other workshop ingredients as you like. Dance 'in the forest' or 'through the looking glass'; move through the chakras and be led by the senses; blindfold the entire group before setting them in motion. I devised a tango project with both blind and sighted performers once where the discipline of the dance steps became a liberation for the visually impaired performers. Be led by different parts of the body; dance in character; above all, enjoy filling the space.

Chapter Twenty-six

ANIMALS AND ARCHETYPES

In the Buddhist monastery of Shaolin, at the foot of Mount Songshan in the Henan Province of China, the monks studied the movements of six creatures and transformed them into performance exercises. The animals were the snake, tiger, bird, bear, deer and monkey. This was long, long ago in the fifth century. Today the monks of Shaolin still use the essence of animal movement in their spectacular martial arts shows with which they tour the world.

The study of animal movement is used in many theatre cultures. In Western traditions it is a training tool to develop observation and physicality. It is also a rehearsal tool: the likening of a character to an animal is often a useful way to rehearse characteristics in performance. In Eastern traditions animals are often the characters themselves. Cambodian classical theatre has four principal characters – the male, the female, the giant and the monkey – which like those of the Italian *commedia dell'arte*, are associated with particular actors throughout their entire careers.

Participants will need to research an animal before starting this workshop. There may be animals outside of the room you are working in. You may need to venture further afield – to a zoo, park, farm or rural area. You might bring a video of animals into the space to work from. The important thing is to use observation as the starting point and then to move beyond it.

Find a space.

Choose an animal.

Become that animal.

Explore your animal body.

How do you move?

How are you articulated?

What is your weight?

Where is your centre of gravity?

What sounds do you make?

How do you breathe?

Explore your environment.

Use all of your senses. Especially the ones that humans do not make full use of.

Smell and taste the world you inhabit.

Feel it with all of your body.

How comfortable does it feel?

Where is it best to be?

How can you hide?

How do you move in the terrain?

Interact with the other animals.

Move through the seasons.

From winter to spring – waking from hibernation, foraging for food.

Spring into summer – warmth, the sun, moulting, nesting, protecting your young and territory.

Summer to autumn – slowing down, food more difficult to find, storage, hibernation and scarcity of food.

Create an environment, a world, as you create the animals, bringing them into the forest or the desert.

Allow as much time as you need to bring these creatures to life. Break and observe them one by one. Discuss what is being done and what is being seen. Work into the depths of the sea and the heights of the sky as is appropriate.

An actor may be asked to play an animal on stage. There was a bear in Théâtre du Soleil's production of Hélène Cixous's *L'Indiade* so convincing that those watching the performance believed it to be real. Robert Holman's play *Other Worlds* tells the true story of a monkey that survived a shipwreck on a remote English coast in the eighteenth century and was mistaken for a Frenchman. The monkey has been a central character in Cambodian classical performance since the first century. Like the other stock characters of Cambodian performance, the monkey is an archetype immediately recognisable by the audience, with strong and unvarying characteristics.

Archetype comes from the Greek word *arketypos* meaning 'first moulded'. An archetypal character in drama is one that is a readily recognisable type, a constantly recurring character. Many theatre cultures are built around archetypes or stock characters. The Italian *commedia dell'arte* is perhaps the best-known European example. The stories of the *commedia dell'arte* were improvised around a group of characters immediately recognisable from their physicality, mannerisms, movements, costumes and masks. Arlecchino (Harlequin) is the comic servant at the centre of the plays. He is a lazy prankster who zigzags around the stage with great agility. Il Capitano (the Captain) is the braggart soldier, a ridiculous coward who thinks himself the swash-buckling hero. He is slow and grand in coming forward, quick at running away. Il Dottore (the Doctor) is the pompous middle-aged man who thinks he knows everything but is the laughing stock at the end of the play. He walks with very small steps. Innamorata (the Lovers) are the embodiment of being in love. They are completely wrapped up in themselves, and self-obsessed, self-regarding. And there is Pantelone, the miserly old merchant, torn between his love for young women and his desire for money.

These were the stock characters we began with in the little African village of Fitches Corner but, as we found there, all cultures have their archetypal characters and they are often similar.

For the next exercise, choose some archetypes. You may want to use those of Cambodia or *commedia*. You might find ones that are more familiar to your group or useful to your purpose. Some, everyone will know – the lover, the hero, the villain, the miser, the glutton, the saint. Others may be more contemporary figures – the celebrity, the city trader, the television evangelist. Give each participant an archetypal character.

Start on the grid.

Move as yourself.

Slow down.

Monitor yourself and your movement.

Gradually take on the characteristics of your archetype.

Start from the feet.

Let the archetype move up through your body.

This is work about extremes, dealing with the physicalisation of the essences of character. Always start from neutral – from the elimination of the character of the performer before building up the archetypal character. Push the work to distort the neutral body, making it do things that it has never done before. Work in detail. Perhaps just the 'foot' of the archetype, or the 'neck' can be worked on in isolation from the rest of the body, but then notice how work on one particular body part will affect all the others. You can apply the work to texts, finding the archetype within a character and playing with it. Romeo and Juliet as the lovers are obvious but what of Hamlet and Ophelia as the lovers, or Gertrude and Claudius, or even Hamlet and Gertrude? The excesses of the *commedia dell'arte* lovers can be used to get to the heart of the transformation of Beatrice and Benedick. You can take the archetype and then add in a line of text. Create Pantelone and give him one of these lines to indicate different aspects of the Pantelone character and also to find Pantelone in different Shakespearean characters:

- 'Strike her young bones with lameness!' says the father to the annoying daughter.
- 'O! help me, help me! Pluck but off these rags, and then death, death!' says the braggadocio pretending to have been robbed.
- 'I spy entertainment in her . . . she gives the leer of invitation,' says the elderly lecher.

These are all characteristics of Pantelone but all very different Shakespearean characters: Lear, Autolycus and Falstaff.

Use the physical to make contact with the truth.

Finish by creating your own improvisation by bringing archetypes together in a relay. Have one character establish themselves in the space and then have another join them. As a third character comes in, one of the others can leave, and so on. Once this is going well, free up the exercise to allow, as with the work in Stepping into Space, any performer to enter the space or to leave it, creating a series of constantly changing situations and tableaux from the stock of characters in the room.

Chapter Twenty-seven

POSTCARD PEOPLE

Our personality, our sexuality, our history, our family, our cultures and our societies all affect the ways in which we use our bodies and demonstrate ourselves to the rest of the world. They affect how we stand, how we hold ourselves, how our bones, joints, muscles all relate to each other and are articulated. They affect how we occupy space and how we move within it. No one has the same personality, sexuality, history, family, culture and society as anyone else. Everyone is different. And it is in that difference that the magic of acting lies. There is an infinite number of different characters with which to people the stage, and an infinite number of possibilities within every different character. Every actor, like Edith Evans, has 'an awful lot of people' inside of themselves. No two actors are the same and so no two Hamlets will ever be the same. It is the actor's job to be every imaginable character, every imaginable being or human being.

Every person has the potential to do anything. Every actor has the potential to play anybody. So any actor should have the potential of becoming anyone doing anything. The transformation of the neutral performer's body to that of any character or creature real or imagined in any situation is the job of acting. I was once asked to choreograph a tango sequence for a production of an English Jacobean tragedy. One of the actors really struggled with the dance, remembering having been told at the age of three that he was a hopeless dancer. For thirty years, that comment had stayed with him and hindered his capabilities both on stage and off. Yet in a workshop when his character was asked to tango, there was no problem at all. The character he played was a splendid tango dancer and showed his skill every night on stage. Only the actor still struggled with the steps.

Marianne Wex's research has shown how the adoption of pose, the creation of identity through the way in which the body is used and the way in which it is dressed has changed over the centuries. The ways in which we perceive ourselves, our bodies, the ways we perceive each other and each other's bodies are ever changing. Studying a period in history enables us to see these changes and to understand our use of our own bodies today, by providing a contrast with how they were used in the past. This workshop explores through study and research different ways in which the human body has been used in the past. The research can be done by the participants or by the workshop leader.

Before the workshop begins, find some picture postcards of paintings of people from a different age or culture. I will use the Elizabethan age as an example. It was the age of Shakespeare, the age in which kings and queens chose their marriage partners through paintings. It was the photography of its day. Of course, not everyone had their portrait painted, so those that survive today are of a particular stratum of society. The pictures we have are of kings and queens, princesses and princes, archetypes who appear in their different forms in drama through every century and in every culture.

Work in groups or in pairs.

Using the postcards as guides, create a man of the period.

Pose one member of the group – or if working in pairs, each other.

First, start with the body in neutral.

Having created neutrality of the performer, begin the transformation.

Again, work methodically from the feet to the top of the head.

Take care over each detail – think about every finger, every vertebra.

Constantly refer back to the postcards.

How is the body posed and presented?

Present the Elizabethan men you have created to each other.

Discuss what you have presented and what you have been shown. Talk about what has worked and what has not. Discuss why these men might have adopted these poses. Why are the feet in those positions? Where are the hands and why? How does the neck relate to the shoulders and the head to the neck? What other differences have been noticed? How difficult or not was this pose to achieve? Now do the same with a portrait of a woman.

Remember that the gender of the performer does not have to be the same as the gender of the person being created.

> Working in groups or in pairs, create a woman of the period.
>
> Begin again with the feet.
>
> Work up through all those bones and joints.
>
> Make the connections.
>
> Through the legs and hips.
>
> Up the spine, across the shoulders and down the arms.
>
> Pay special attention to the hands.
>
> Then the neck and the placing of the head upon it.
>
> Work out the relation of each part of the body to the others.
>
> What is facing front and what to which side?
>
> Think about the breathing even though you cannot see it.
>
> Where is the gaze?

We have just done poses. Posing for a portrait is not a natural activity. Discuss why these poses have been adopted, how close to or far from reality they might be. Talk about the representation of gender in the poses and what might be learned from that. Then start to walk.

> Return to your groups/pairs and put in movement.
>
> Start with your men and assume the pose.
>
> Make any changes that you think necessary after your discussions.
>
> Now walk your character.
>
> Like the bunraku puppets, he may need help.
>
> Work out what are the essentials of the pose that are going to affect the walking.
>
> Find out how much of the pose is a frozen moment that can be unfrozen into movement.
>
> Bring the group together and have all the Elizabethan men walk in the space.
>
> Ask them to greet each other.

Find time to discuss what has been done, what is essential to period, character and status. Then do the same exercise with the female portraits.

> Let the women move to one side of the space and the men to the other.
>
> Now all inhabit the space together.
>
> Greet each other and pass by.
>
> Then add in the voice.

How does the use of the body affect the use of the voice?

Having played with these, you can have fun with grandmother's footsteps and apply this to Elizabethan physicality. Apply the Elizabethan men and women to specific characters in a particular moment in a Shakespeare play, Macbeth and Lady Macbeth, say, at their coronation, or Gertrude and Claudius at their wedding. Perhaps Viola and Rosalind making their transitions to Cesario and Ganymede.

You are creating a particular world and culture in a particular time. Any of the workshops can now be used in a period-specific way. This same workshop can be done with any period and with any culture. It can be made specific to a play. In that case, find pictures that suggest ways in which characters might have looked or held themselves, used their bodies and presented themselves to the world. Trawl through books and magazines relevant to the period and culture you are exploring.

This exercise then is a useful way into an exploration of period. I have used it in this particular form to explore gender roles in Shakespeare with schoolchildren from all over Southern Africa. I have used it to discover a visual and performance style for medieval mystery plays and to access the very different world from which those plays came. The paintings of medieval and early Renaissance Europe bring us different characters from the kings and queens of Shakespeare's day. This is a world of one God and of angels, saints and sinners. The carvings on the temples of Angkor Wat in Cambodia bring us a different world of many gods and monkeys and mighty warriors. All are icons, windows into different worlds.

Sometimes it will be impossible for one performer to create

everything represented in the picture. It is from this that our nomad actor Richard Auckland had the idea of 'The Big Frock'.

Take a postcard of one of the Elizabethan women. To have been worthy subjects for a painting, women in Shakespeare's day had to be especially grand, even more so than the men. Their clothes were often big beyond belief. For this workshop, the performers will become not just the character but everything she is wearing.

THE BIG FROCK

Work as one group.

One of you is the person that is the subject of the painting.

As before, create the pose of your character.

The rest of you are her costume.

Create the frock.

Some of you are the heavy skirt, pulling down on either side.

One or more is the corset, tightening the waist.

Some are the heavy shoulders.

Two of you might be the ruff holding the head.

Perhaps others are cuffs, or jewellery, or whatever else you might see in the painting.

Now try and breathe.

Now try and walk.

All the world *is* a stage but more importantly for us the stage can be all the worlds it is possible to imagine. Theatre is about creation and re-creation. You can use any visual material in this workshop. The stone carvings of Ankgor Wat in Cambodia, medieval frescos, rock carvings in Africa or Australia. Create the poses and then begin to move, the performers on their own or manipulated as puppets, and walk any world into existence.

Chapter Twenty-eight

PLAYING WITH GENDER

'We wish you were our husbands!' It was the opening night of *Macbeth* and the nomads were in a town called Glasov in the Udmurt Republic of the Russian Federation, twenty-four hours on the trans-Siberian train from Moscow, cold and isolated on the edge of the Ural Mountains.

The Nomads who were playing the roles of Macbeth and Banquo caused quite a stir in Glasov and for many of the women in the audience they came to be regarded as the perfect men. So it should have come as no surprise after the first performance to find our lead actors fêted, bought drinks and have every kind of proposal made to them by the young women of this small town in the middle of nowhere. It should not have been a surprise, except that our actors were women and not men. Edda Sharpe was our Macbeth and Becky Hall our Banquo. There, in temperatures that plummeted to minus forty degrees Centigrade, they were the hottest men in town.

Eugenio Barba has speculated that behind the disguises of theatrical cross-dressing, what he calls 'the contrast between reality and fiction', lies hidden one of the theatre's 'secret potentialities'. Barba says that within each man there is a woman and within each woman there is a man.

Much of my work has investigated these secret potentialities, which are at the heart of theatrical practice in many cultures. When those first Japanese sailors arrived in London in 1611, as Shakespeare's new play *The Tempest* was opening at the Globe, women were forbidden to appear on the stage. All the parts were written for, and played by, men. It was less than fifty years later that the first female actor appeared on an English stage, as Desdemona in a revival of Shakespeare's *Othello*. On first seeing a woman on stage at around this time, when the London theatres reopened after a period of closure by the Puritans, Samuel Pepys commented in his diaries on how unconvincing her performance was. He did not believe that a woman actor could be as believable or convincing playing a woman on stage as a man actor could. The

King disagreed and shortly afterwards the representation of women by men on the English stage was banned by Parliament. Around the same time in Japan the opposite was happening. There the tradition of women actors playing women on stage ended as the shogunate banned the playing of female roles by women.

Issues around the performance of gender remain at the heart of theatrical practice. In many theatre cultures, cross-dressing in performance is the accepted dominant convention. The English and Scottish traditions of all-male performance survive in the pantomime where the lead female character, the 'dame', is always played by a man, a tradition that extends back through Juliet's nurse into the very roots of British drama. In India, the male actors who play the female parts are called 'singing boys'. There are newer traditions. In Japan, the hugely popular Takarazuka began as recently as 1914. Women play all the parts, both male and female, in lavish musical revues centred around a giant staircase.

TRANSFORMING GENDER

Walk on the grid.

As you walk, your body will gradually change gender.

Male to female.

Female to male.

Feel the difference across your chest.

And in your groin.

Are there changes in your neck and chin?

The way you hold your head?

Feel the change in your hips and in your lips.

And from your hips down to your feet.

How does your walk change?

And your occupancy of the space?

How do you turn on the corners of the grid?

Here your instructions are rather in the form of questions, suggesting areas of change by questioning whether they are happening.

You may need to give a great deal of detail or just a few suggestions. You might want to concentrate on, say, the hands or feet or chest. You might want to work on breathing or on the senses as well as posture. Encourage subtlety and detail. In the previous Postcard People workshop we worked from the outside in. This time, work from the inside out. Suggest interior changes of thought and attitude, leading to exterior changes of stance, posture and movement. What is essentially different?

All the 'women' sit out and watch the 'men'.

This can be done on the grid or as a 'catwalk' show.

Swap over and have the 'men' observe the 'women'.

This will inevitably be amusing and raise many issues not just about acting but about sexuality, sexual politics, and the way in which men and women observe and think about each other and therefore how they represent each other. Spend time discussing all these issues.

How does acting depend on observation, socialisation, shorthand and stereotyping? Where is the archetype beneath? Now it is time to add in the dynamics of interaction and the specifics of situation.

Let's start with the 'men'.

Return to the grid and walk the room.

Greet each other as you meet.

Perhaps you might have a specific social occasion, a party, say. You might add in details of age and social status. It could be a birthday party or a retirement event.

Swap over and have the 'men' observe the 'women'.

Again, take time to stop and discuss what has been performed and what has been observed. What was convincing, what unconvincing and why? Where are the differences? What has to do with physiology? What to do with the social aspects of gender? What is truth and where is the archetype?

Return to the grid.

Walk as your 'gender other'.

Think of a name for yourself as you walk.

Perhaps some history.

Walk to the side of the space.

Place a chair in the middle of the space.

One by one, walk to the chair, sit down, tell us your name, stand and return to the side of the space.

This exercise can then be developed in a series of improvised social situations, perhaps a party, perhaps at work. The nomads used it with great success in South Africa at a schools congress where groups of young people from all over the country had come together to develop their performance skills. Teenagers from many different cultural backgrounds joined the nomads and other professional actors from Southern Africa to find out about themselves, each other and to extend their acting skills through the use of this exercise.

Shakespeare wrote in a world that was without female actors. There was no such word in his London as 'actress'. Throughout all his stage works he plays with the construction of gender through acting and the confusions that can result when biological sex is concealed by both the actor and the character they are playing. Viola in *Twelfth Night* makes the audience complicit in this when she shares with them the realisation that her 'outside' has 'charmed' Olivia. Like Viola, the part of Rosalind in *As You Like It* was conceived for a male actor pretending to be a female character who then herself pretends to be a man, Ganymede. When the play has finished, Rosalind, or rather the actor playing Rosalind, comes forward and addresses the audience:

> It is not the fashion to see the lady the epilogue; but it is no more unhandsome than to see the lord the prologue. If it be true that good wine needs no bush, 'tis true that a good play needs no epilogue. Yet to good wine they do use good bushes; and good plays prove the better by the help of good epilogues. What a case am I in, then, that am neither a good epilogue, nor cannot insinuate with you in the behalf of a

good play! I am not furnish'd like a beggar; therefore to beg
will not become me. My way is to conjure you; and I'll begin
with the women. I charge you, O women, for the love you
bear to men, to like as much of this play as please you; and I
charge you, O men, for the love you bear to women – as I
perceive by your simpering none of you hates them – that
between you and the women the play may please. If I were a
woman, I would kiss as many of you as had beards that
pleased me, complexions that liked me, and breaths that I
defied not; and, I am sure, as many as have good beards, or
good faces, or sweet breaths, will, for my kind offer, when I
make curtsy, bid me farewell.

Working in groups of three, give your actors the freedom to find a
way of presenting this speech to the rest of the participants in
whatever way they choose, so as to bring out as many of the
paradoxes as they are able and so release what Barba calls those
'secret potentialities'.

Chapter Twenty-nine
CLOTHING

John Gielgud, the British actor, once said that until he got the shoes right he was never confident in his performance. Clothing is about the externals of character, but all clothing represents a choice and is therefore an expression of character. Why do we wear what we wear? Why do we choose the clothes we do and feel more comfortable in some than in others? What do the externals of apparel say about the internals of character? How does clothing alter how we use our bodies, how we think about them and how we think about ourselves? Does clothing affect thought and action as well as appearance? The possibilities with clothing in workshops and performances are many and varied.

This workshop can be done without any preparation using whatever your participants happen to be wearing that day, but thought and decision-making by the participants in the days before the workshop will produce much better results. This is the simple instruction ideally given at the end of the previous workshop so as to allow time to prepare a starting point for this one:

> Bring to the space a piece of clothing to which you have a sentimental attachment.

This can be any piece of clothing. It can be something that is regularly worn or something that has not been worn for years. The important thing is that whoever has it in their possession has a reason, however slight and unformed, for keeping it. The items should be brought in bags so as not to be seen by the other participants before the workshop starts. When everyone is in the room with their piece of clothing, give the following simple instruction:

> Using anywhere in the space and any methods of your choice, create a way of presenting your piece of clothing to the group. You have twenty minutes.

This may be enough instruction, or you may have to reinforce the idea with suggestions. It may be that someone will choose simply to stand in front of the group and say what the garment is and tell something about it. It may be that someone will choose just to wear their garment. Some people may need the help of one, more or all of their colleagues. Encourage thought about audience, the use of space and of the relationship between performance space and audience space. Many of the concepts that have been explored in previous workshops can come into play in this very simple exercise.

It may be that you give the participants the freedom to go outside of the workshop room, into other parts of the building or into the open air. It may be that you restrict the amount of time allowed for the exercise. Inevitably, some participants will come up with an idea very quickly. Others will take more time. Some ideas may require considerable preparation, others none at all. Monitor everyone closely so as to be able to offer support, help with difficulties and keep an eye on progress so as to know when everyone, or at least most people, are ready to show. There will always be some who require, or think they require, extra time. Give a five-minute warning before the time is up, and then a two-minute one.

When the time is right, everyone shows what they have prepared. Be ready for revelation and surprise. Some may make complete solo performances with the clothing as a catalyst. Others may involve other members of the group in their performances. When everyone has shown, spend time on questions and discussion. This discussion is important. What is it that makes a piece of clothing important or gives it its significance? Clothing can go to the very heart and soul of a person or a character. It can relate to the way they use their bodies, sense the world and relate to their chakras. The exercise can be applied to the creation of character, giving the actor and thereby the character, ownership of what they wear so that it is transformed from mere costume to clothing.

Sometimes costume is important and should be 'owned' by the performer and the character they are playing so as to become not a costume but clothing. Sometimes costume is vital to the telling of the story. When Viola dresses as a boy on the beach of Illyria, what clothes does she dress in? Does she borrow them from the sailors? Does she buy new garments? Perhaps she has found clothes washed up on the beach. Are they the clothes of the brother she believes to have been drowned?

This simple exercise of showing a piece of personal clothing can be developed in many ways – I have created entire performances from it. It can also be used as a way of introducing members of a new ensemble to each other. In one variation the exercise can be a good way of exploring a recent period, asking actors to find from their home or their families or a charity/thrift shop a piece of clothing specific to a year or decade.

A collaborator on almost every project I have worked on has been the administrator Liz Turner. While we were working in Brighton one year, she came across an extraordinary pair of shoes in a charity shop. She could not resist buying them, telling me she was sure that a workshop could be devised around them. The shoes were made of black and red leather, with a strong heel, but most unusually were 'cloven' at the front, which gave them a strange, devilish quality. The shoes were placed in the middle of the circle of actors. Whoever wore the shoes became taken over by the evil within them. The transformations were horrible and subtle. Some wrestled physically with the shoes, desperately trying to remove them once they realised what was happening. One actor simply offered a biscuit to each of the others, with a gentle smile.

This exercise can also be done with objects. The power of the prop is immense. No object should be on stage without a good reason. Any object used by the actor then takes on great significance almost to the extent of becoming an additional performer. Some theatre traditions use few props or none at all. In Chinese opera a table and two chairs are used to depict every kind of location, status and situation. A chair can be a well or a table a mountain top. Any object can carry significance from the way in which it is used on stage and the associations actors and audience bring to it. Have everyone bring an object into the workshop that holds a significant meaning for them. Again give them time and a simple instruction and have them present the object to the group.

The most moving experience I have had using this exercise was not with a group of actors but with a group of business people from a company that was sponsoring a play I was working on. The company felt that too many of their employees were working in isolation from each other and asked me to run a drama workshop that would help them find out about each other and create bonds within the workforce. With this sentimental object work everyone, all from very different parts of the organisation and at different levels of management, revealed things to their colleagues that were unknown and unexpected. One middle manager in his late fifties brought in a photograph of his school rugby team with himself pictured in the group. He asked all his colleagues in the workshop to recreate the photograph. Benches were brought in and the photograph was studied closely. The group cast themselves as each of the rugby players. There was banter and camaraderie, much as there must have been when the photograph was taken. The moment of the taking of the photograph was recreated and everyone smiled for the imaginary camera. Then the man whose photograph it was asked the group to hold the pose. One by one he removed people from the recreated photograph. Eventually a handful were left. The man whose photograph it was went one by one around those he had removed from the photograph. He named each of them and told us how and when they had died since the photograph was taken.

As with the clothing, this exercise can be applied to character and give the performer ownership of another part of the creative theatrical process. Every object used on stage should be as rich with significance and history as the office worker's photograph. The word 'history' comes from the Greek *historein* meaning 'to narrate', and every prop should contain a story within it. Ophelia's flowers, Hamlet's books and Prospero's, Desdemona's handkerchief, Rosalind's curtle axe, Macbeth's dagger, Shylock's turquoise ring and the ring Olivia gives to Viola, and everything in Winnie's bag as she sits up to her waist in the sand, all should have the possibility of performance themselves.

Chapter Thirty

MAGIC SILKS

I was in the Russian Market in Phnom Penh when I found the magic silks. I was looking for fabrics for the nomads' production of *Pericles*, Shakespeare's late play of gods and romance, sudden death and unexpected life, tenderness and debauchery, love and reconciliation. The narrow alleyways of the market were full of silks of every imaginable colour, enough to dress any conceivable play. I chose just six, as many as there were to be actors in the production. Back in London, the silks became perfect stimuli for an exploration of some of the themes of the play.

If suggestion is about the evocation of thoughts, feelings and memories in the mind, stimulation is about arousal through the senses. Performers can be stimulated in all sorts of ways and the stimulation can be of their minds, their bodies or their emotions. Sometimes it is possible to stimulate and suggest all three at the same time with the same object. In the *Pericles* workshops each of the Cambodian silks took on a different aspect of the play. The black silk was death. The purple silk was kingship. Cream represented innocence, green jealousy, grey evil, and the pink silk erotic love. You do not have to travel to Cambodia to find cloths. You can use scarves, handkerchiefs or whatever comes to hand, and you can use as few or as many colours as you choose. You will also need a God, chosen from among your performers.

There are magic pieces of silk in the room.

And there is a God.

Find a space and begin to walk on the grid.

God can give you a silk or place one on you at any time.

As the silk is placed or given, react to its qualities and its colour.

Interact with the silk; move with it; clothe yourself in it. Let it feed your imagination. If God changes the silk, respond to the new qualities and colour.

I chose colours to represent different themes we had found in the play. Fate was a further theme, hence the intervention in the workshop of a 'God' figure. You could just as easily manipulate the silks yourself as workshop leader. An advantage of silks or similar cloths is that they can be used in many different ways. Their colours may be suggestive and their physical presence may stimulate the mind and body in a variety of ways. They will encourage intervention. The randomness and juxtaposition of their appearance and their continual changing will lead to rapid reactions and responses.

The associated emotion, status or role given to the silks acts as a trigger in the same way that the pieces of paper do in the Box of Emotions workshop. The silks are tactile and can be functional. They will become ever-changing costumes and props. They can be worn and played with. They can be put into contact with other silks and with other performers. They can be placed on the floor or waved in the air, used as turbans, shawls or shrouds. They can be hidden behind, lain on or fondled and caressed.

The colours have significances beyond those attributed by the workshop leader and can themselves stimulate and suggest. As Jo King, director of the London School of Striptease once said to me, 'Colours press buttons.' Different colours will press different buttons and signify different things in different cultures. The colour of death is black throughout Europe but is white in Japan. In Islam, green is the colour of wisdom while in the Christian world it is more often associated with youth and renewal. Red is good luck for the Chinese but also the colour of communism and anarchy. For Cambodians it is the colour of the Khmer Rouge. The colour attributions I chose were for the most part traditional European ones. I could have just used black and white or black, white and red. If you are exploring a design schema for a production, introduce the elements of that schema through this workshop.

The coloured silks make suggestions to the mind and stimulate the senses. They are tactile and visual, make sounds, and even have a smell and a taste. With their suggestions, performers will work on both a conscious and an unconscious level.

Colours also work with the chakras. Red is associated with the root chakra, orange with the spleen, yellow with the solar plexus, green with the heart, blue with the throat, indigo with the 'third eye' and violet with the crown. You could make physical associations with your silks rather than emotional ones in this way, add in the senses too, or make any number of combinations.

A silk cloth is one of the Nang-mchod, the Offerings of the Five Senses in Tibetan Buddhist ceremonies. Offerings are made to please the senses of tranquil deities. The piece of silk pleases the sense of touch. The offering of a mirror pleases the sense of form, or sight. A bell or stringed musical instrument is for hearing. The deities' sense of smell is pleased with offerings of incense, nutmeg or scented flowers. A special sacrificial cake, Gto-Ma, or perhaps sugar, or a conch filled with sweetmeats is offered for the sense of taste.

Stimulant objects, images and sounds are for me a favourite way of starting a workshop or a rehearsal process. The elements can be contributed by the workshop leaders or by the participants.

One of my favourite memories of object stimulation, though, started on the seashore of the little English town of Deal. Noël Greig was about to write a play for Theatre Nomad. The play would eventually become *At Break of Day*. At this stage one of the few things Noël and I knew was that much of the play would take place at night and deal with dreams and things of the dark. We also knew that the play would involve borders and the crossing of them. So for the first workshop at which Noël was to meet the actors for whom he was writing and the collaborators with whom he would be working, we decided to meet on the coast of Kent where he and I had done so many projects over the years. With a clear autumn sky it was possible to see the lights of France twinkling across the Channel. The cast had not met before. All were asked to arrive at a point on the beach at dusk with a sentimental object hidden in a pocket and the memory of a dream and a night-time experience that they could recount to the rest of the group. It was cold when we all met up. Darkness was drawing in and the tide was high. The sounds of waves breaking on the shingle drowned much of our conversation. Noël gave an instruction. We were all to go and find an object on the beach. It could be anything. We went off and combed the beach and when we had returned, all walked the short distance to a small and cosy church hall lit with dozens of candles placed there by our administrator Liz Turner. A long roll of paper stretched from one end of the hall to the other. Through the night we told our stories and recounted our dreams. We showed the objects brought from our homes and collected from the beach, and as midnight passed and the candles burned low Noël listened to all that we said and did and acted and to the myriad stories that were recounted. The long roll of paper became covered in notes, a written record of the workshop. All of us in the room added to it our own thoughts and ideas. Somewhere in all the words and actions was a narrative waiting to be found.

Chapter Thirty-one
ONCE UPON A TIME

'All you need to make theatre,' said Athol Fugard, 'is three things: an actor, a space and a pair of ears.' Noël Greig describes the essence of theatre as being 'one actor on a bare platform inhabiting two worlds simultaneously'. For Fugard and Greig, acting at its most basic is about one person telling a story to another. Beyond that, as it becomes one group of people telling stories to another group of people, the difference is only a matter of scale. As we come towards the end of this book it is time to begin to tell stories. Perhaps it will be the story of the play you are rehearsing that you want to tell; perhaps you might want to invent stories. The South African poet Looks Matoto once said to me, 'Everyone has a story to tell.' Your workshop space will be full of stories, and full of performers able to tell them. They can be told with words that all in the room can understand. They can be told with words that no one in the room can understand. They can be told by one person or by many. They can be told with movements of the body or with movements of just parts of the body, as Karola and my feet told a scene from *Hamlet* in Eugenio Barba's workshop. They can be told with sounds or with silence. This workshop explores ways of finding the stories in the room and finding ways of telling those stories.

'Once upon a time . . .' is a good way to start. It is an English phrase but has an equivalent in every language. The French say, '*Il etais une fois . . .*' In Xhosa it is something similar, '*Kwathi ke kaloku ngabali . . .*' My favourite way to start is in Hungarian, where children are told, '*Egyszer volt hol nem volt (az üveghegyen innen), az óperenciás tengeren tú . . .*' which means something like, 'Once there was (where there wasn't), somewhere beyond the sea . . .' At the end of this workshop you will be able to say that you have created something where once there wasn't.

This first exercise uses the entire group to create a story. It is very simple.

THE PEBBLE AND THE FIRE

Form a circle in the room, as if you were around a fire.

Imagine the flames dancing in front of you.

There is a pebble in the middle of the circle.

We are going to tell a story.

Anyone can take the pebble and begin.

Begin with the words 'Once upon a time'.

When you feel you have told your bit of the story, place the pebble back in the centre of the circle.

Anyone can pick up the pebble and carry on.

When one story is finished, another can start.

The magic-story pebble came from that devising process on the beach in Deal with Noël Greig and can be used in many ways. You do not need a pebble. Sometimes I have used a small carpet in the middle of the circle on which the storyteller sits to tell their tale. I have used a model ship that travels from person to person. You might find an object that is suited to your particular project. A shell is a useful object. It holds memories and sounds within it, which will be recalled when it is held to the ear. The advantage of a pebble is that it can be easily passed around. Its tactile qualities act like prayer or worry beads, aiding concentration. The continual return of the pebble to the centre provides a focus but also allows for spontaneity. Anyone can intervene in the story. No one is sitting anxiously knowing that, if the story moves around the circle, they have to come up with something to follow their neighbour. This method also keeps the story constantly open. There may be improvisatory riffs. Anything could happen. All playmaking should be like that. Every performance of *Macbeth* should be telling the story as if for the first time. Perhaps Macbeth will not kill Duncan. Perhaps Lady Macbeth will not convince her husband that he can become king. Every turning point in the play is just one of an infinity of possibilities. Each decision made by a character is the flutter of a butterfly's wing in the chaos of the world of the play. Even the smallest character can have as great an influence. If the messenger hesitates in bringing the letter from Macbeth to his wife, things will be different. A friend of mine was watching a performance of *Macbeth* on Broadway. Christopher Plummer and Glenda Jackson were the stars. As the audience left at the end of the play, his elderly neighbour turned to his wife and said, 'Gee, surprise ending.' Every ending should be a surprise, however many times a play has been performed. Every moment within the play should hold open a multitude of possible plot turns.

Try this exercise with the story of a play you are working on. Tell the story of *Twelfth Night*, say. Anyone in the play can start telling the story but should tell it from the point of view of their character. Perhaps Orsino will start – as he does in the play. Maybe it will be Sir Toby or Maria. Perhaps it will be the Sea Captain or Sebastian. As the pebble moves around the group, the story will be revealed like a multifaceted jewel, seen from many angles, and containing a multitude of different stories within itself.

In creating new stories or retelling old ones, they can be of any length. One person may tell the entire story without anyone else picking up the pebble. Someone may add only a detail. Everyone may be involved in the telling or just a few of the group.

THE BURNING MATCH

Try it with a box of matches instead of a pebble. Whoever picks up the box has to strike a match and can only talk until the match has burned down. You might ask for an entire story to be told before the match has burned or the life story of the person holding the match. This is quite difficult to do. Try it with the story of the play. Actors have to tell the story in the length of time it takes for their match to burn down.

This is a wonderful way of getting to the heart of a play. 'What is a play about?' people will ask, expecting to be answered with themes and ideas and concepts. But a play is simply a story and this exercise can help you find its essential elements.

Now we will move on to individual stories. These can be linked by theme, character, location and so on, or simply told for themselves. Again use the pebble, or your equivalent, as the trigger for the story.

Sit in a circle as if around a campfire.

Tell a story to the rest of the group.

Whoever has the pebble can tell their tale.

Return the pebble to the centre when you have finished.

This exercise takes us back to the beginning of the voice work. It is as much about listening as it is about speaking. If you are lucky, you will have a group with many different mother tongues. If so, ask each person to tell the story in their mother tongue, whether or not anyone else in the group can speak that language. Now the clarity of the storytelling and the concentration of the listening become acute. I have done this with groups where the languages have been as different as Japanese, Xhosa and Hungarian. There is always a way of communicating the story.

The final exercise returns to working in pairs.

YOUR PARTNER'S STORY

Find a partner.

Tell each other a true personal story: something that has happened to you.

Find something that is universal. I have found that this exercise works well with a 'best' or 'worst' scenario. In devising the Marylebone station performance, we used 'my best or my worst Christmas' as a starting point. The material we generated was not used as text in the final performance but as the starting point of creating a movement-based piece of work. For the Nomads' Casanova show all the performers were asked to recount their most unusual or funniest sexual experience. In Theatre Nomad's play about Joan of Arc, *La Pucelle*, the four actresses told stories of experiences when they were the age at which Joan heard her voices.

Now tell the rest of the group your partner's story.

In the first person.

As if you were your partner.

This transference of the ownership of the story can be fascinating, releasing all sorts of possibilities. There are a multiplicity of choices to be made here about both characterisation and story-telling and the exercise can get to the very heart of acting and impersonation. Everything that we have done can be brought to bear on the simple task of being somebody else and telling his or her story.

You can adapt many of the previous workshops to the task of storytelling. You can tell a story as blind man's buff or using the hopscotch board. You can use each vertebra as a link in the story, or each footstep. You can tell the story with a drum or in a labyrinth. You can tango the story with danger, sex and passion. You can use the box of emotions to give a different colour to every part of the story as it is told. You can use silks and sexual stimulants. Like Chinese whispers, the story will be ever changing.

Chapter Thirty-two

PERFORMANCE

Your workshop room is as full of stories as Prospero's isle is full of noises. Many tales were told in the previous workshop. Many others have been touched on in all of the workshops that have gone before. Some were personal and true, some were fanciful; some were folk tales and some were made up collectively by the group; some were stories from plays you know or are working on; some were contained in sonnets, songs or childhood rhymes. In this final workshop of the programme, choose one of these stories to tell through performance by the entire group. I have chosen *Macbeth* to use as my example, but the process will work with any play or story known collectively by the workshop participants.

A STORY IN PERFORMANCE

Start by recalling your story. Pass the magic pebble around the group or have a ball thrown from person to person. Minds should be concentrated on the story. Tell it as many times as you need until it is owned by the entire group.

Once you have your story, decide who will play which characters. If just one or two of you have been working through the programme on your own, you will have to play every part between you, from Macbeth and Lady Macbeth to the drunken Porter and the advancing Burnham Wood. If you have a large group, you can cast as many parts as you are able and are essential to the telling of the story. You might dispense with Hecate and reduce your murderers to one. You might have enough performers to cast all of your apparitions or you might leave them in the mind's eye. You might decide to double up rather than lose characters completely.

Now that you have your story and a cast of characters you must decide how to use your space. As we begin the transition from workshop to performance, think of your audience and where they will be.

Open up one or more of your walls to the listening and seeing world outside. This may be done collectively or by you as the workshop leader. It is an important decision and should be done with careful thought. The space that is the performers' must be carefully defined. The realm of the audience must be clearly separated. You might decide to play in the round and open up all of the walls. Be crystal clear as to what is the domain of performance and at which points the actors are in their performing space and at which points they are out of it. Walk the grid to establish every part of the performance floor.

Recalling the story and establishing the grid are the beginnings of a warm-up. Now it is important to warm up the body in detail, starting with a stretch. Take time over this, limbering the bodies of the performers so that they are ready to recap all of the workshops of the programme and apply them to the story they are about to tell.

Stretch.

Start with the feet.

Work in detail on all those bones and joints and find a point of grounding and balance.

Build up through the body, up through the spine and down into the tips of the fingers.

Reach a point of magic neutrality.

Inhabit the space with your body.

Work your way comfortably and with the least effort around the room.

Breathe as you walk.

Deep into your body.

Inspire and expire.

Float open 'ahs' on your out-breaths.

None of this should be rushed and the work should be done as deeply as it was in the original workshop. Constantly monitor the individuals within the group and the ensemble as a whole to ensure that magic neutrality is achieved by all and that breathing is relaxed and even. Only when you are certain that this has been achieved should you move on and introduce characters to the performers' bodies.

Become stationary.

Let your characters begin to inhabit your neutral body, throwing you off balance as they take you over, from your feet up through your legs, into your torso and spine, up into your neck and head and down into your hands and fingers.

Do this slowly in detail, working up through the body.

Don't rush.

Let your character inhabit your neutral body.

Have your character put your body into motion.

Work on an action your character is doing with your body: Lady Macbeth washing her hands, Macbeth prevaricating over the murder of Duncan, Banquo realising Macbeth's treachery. It can be something central to the story you are telling or something quite ordinary.

Return to the grid and to movement.

Reinhabit the space with your characters: witches on a blasted heath, Lady Macbeth alone with her letter at Inverness, Lady Macduff anxiously at home with her children.

Make patterns on the floor.

This is a lot to achieve. As always, do not allow your performers to rush. Allow discovery and transformation to happen gently, gradually and with the detail of truth. Only when physicality is fully achieved can we move on to voice.

Notice how your breathing is changing as your character takes over your body.

Think of a line or two, perhaps just a word, from the story you are in: 'Tomorrow and tomorrow and tomorrow'; 'Unsex me here'; 'Knock, knock, knock.'

Put the words on your breath as you move.

Listen for a rhythm and move to it as you trace patterns in the room.

Body, voice and character should now be coming together. Characters should be growing, developing in the room, filling the space with sound and with movement as they travel. Every square centimetre of the grid, every cubic centimetre of the air above it, should be filled with the patterns and noises of the play. Once this is achieved you can add relationships to the dynamics in the room.

> You have been working on your own.
>
> Become aware that you are not on your own.
>
> You are in a world full of the other characters of the play.
>
> React to other characters as you come across them.

Allow time for this to be played with and explored. Every character should have an opportunity to interact with every other.

> Return to silence.
>
> Slowly come to a stop.
>
> Listen to your breathing.
>
> We are ready to work through the senses.

Work through them one by one: touch, hearing, smell, taste, sight and intuition. Lady Macbeth listening to a knocking and the owl's shriek. Macbeth seeing the dagger before him. A servant feeling the cold floor of the castle beneath their feet. The witches sensing the arrival of Banquo and Duncan on the blasted heath. Members of the court tasting the food as Macbeth sees Banquo's ghost. Macduff smelling the blood as he discovers Duncan's body. Do the same exercise with the chakras, working from the base through to the crown.

We are now ready to begin the journeys contained in the play. Each character has their own.

> Take yourself through the labyrinthine journey of the story as your character knows it, twisting and turning on every development.
>
> Find what is at the centre of your character's labyrinth. The murder of Duncan or the crowning of Macbeth? The killing of Macduff's family or the Porter's opening of the door? Bringing Macbeth's letter to Lady Macbeth? Murdering or being murdered?

The labyrinth here is a solo exercise with characters finding their own personal journeys. Follow it by returning to the development of relationships in the room. Set up a tango salon with chairs at either side of the space. Play some music.

> Tango.
>
> Macbeth and Banquo with each other and then with the witches.
>
> Then Banquo on his own as Macbeth tangos into the arms of Lady Macbeth with her leading his steps.
>
> Duncan might dance with Macbeth and Banquo might cut in.
>
> Lady Macbeth might dance with the memory of her father.
>
> The Gentlewoman might tango with the Doctor.

Allow for every possible combination. Some will be unexpected. Every character will have a relationship with every other. Some relationships will be close and intimate, some will be limited and cursory. All will be able to be expressed on the dance floor. When the music stops have everyone return to their seat at the side of the space. We will return again to solo work.

> Choose an emotion that will consume you: Banquo's honesty, Lady Macbeth's ambition, Lady Macduff's protectiveness, Duncan's decisiveness.
>
> Work the emotion on a scale with precision and control as it completely takes you over.

Work this slowly. Allow the emotion to grow from the inside out. It can help to find a chakra as the physical centre from which the all-consuming emotion will grow. Once this work is established on the chairs, allow your actors freedom of movement in the space and allow them to interact with the other emotions and characters in the room. Then let the emotions dissipate and the actors return to their seats.

Lastly, bring in object work. All performers should have an object or a piece of clothing to help tell their story and to make suggestions to them and the rest of the group: a dagger, or a bowl of water, or a letter, throne or crown. It should be brought in for the workshop.

In character, show your object or piece of clothing to the other
characters in your story.

Give more time to those parts of the programme which seem most
appropriate to the story you are telling, but be methodical in
working through the body and voice, and take care to monitor for
balance and neutrality before character and story begin to
intervene. This will be even more important if your performers are
doubling parts. In that case, repeat exercises for different
characters but always return to neutral in between, using the grid
and monitoring your performers.

Now we can tell our story.

Use all that you can of all the exercises you have just done.

Use as few or as many words as you need.

Fill the space with your characters and with their story.

Be as clear as you can.

Be essential.

Walk on the grid until you are at ease and neutral.

Find your space in the room.

Face the world outside and perform your story.

We have finished with the essence of theatre. A group of people
telling a story with just themselves, their bodies and their voices,
their hearts and their souls as the tools of communication. We
have moved from workshop to performance.

Epilogue

Once upon a time, I met a holy man from Senegal. He talked to me about God. 'There is only one truth,' he said, 'but there are many different doors to that truth.'

I was reminded of these words as I finished writing this book. The diversity of these workshops comes from my good fortune to have had experiences as a director and teacher in many cultures and in many corners of the globe. They have been informed by my travels and by the other directors and teachers I have met with and worked with along the way. The further I have travelled and the more theatre makers I have met, the more convinced I have become that in our more secular world, the words of the holy man from Senegal equally apply.

From the *favelas* of Brazil to the townships of Southern Africa, from jungle clearings in Cambodia to church halls in England, from proscenium stages in North America to *hanamichi* in Japan, wherever we are making theatre, whatever style of theatre it may be and from whichever culture it may come, we are all of us through our different doors searching for ways to reveal truth through performance.

Enjoy, as I have, exploring the world of theatre and its many cultures as you open the doors of these workshops. Good luck in finding many other doors of your own.

Theatre Nomad brings together theatre makers from around the world working in a variety of theatrical traditions to reinterpret classic texts and create new theatre for new audiences and new situations. The company began life in London as 'the soho group' but now spends its life travelling the world. As part of its commitment to the exploration of performance, the company has run workshops on Shakespeare in the townships of South Africa, on trance performance in England, on the acting of gender in North America, and on text and theatre skills in schools and colleges across Europe. The company has performed in the Shakespeare Gardens in Paris, high up in the Bavarian Alps, in a ruined church as part of the International Shakespeare Festival in Gdansk, at the Hong Kong City Festival and across South Africa. For more information see www.theatrenomad.com.

The **International Workshop Festival** is a UK-based organisation established in 1988 to provide continuing training and educational opportunities in the performing arts. Festivals are presented each year in London with workshops, talks, presentations and demonstrations for professional performing artists. The workshops are led by practitioners and teachers internationally renowned in their particular field and come from a variety of performing arts disciplines and backgrounds. The IWF also publishes the online World Directory of Performance Training (www.workshopfestival.co.uk).